ADVANCE PRAISE

"Business relationships have historically been made on a balance of partial truths and intentional omissions. That is exactly why businesses struggle to grow. In this book, you will discover how to leverage raw honesty to make more sales and retain more clients than ever before. Your business is about to be transformed—honestly."

—**MIKE MICHALOWICZ**, author of *Get Different* and *Profit First*

"Vulnerability creates connection, and Matt's message is one that all entrepreneurs should take to heart and implement in their business, especially in today's business landscape. *Painted Baby* hits the nail on the head in terms of how to do this effectively in your business."

—**JAIME MASTERS**, *Eventual Millionaire*

"*Painted Baby* is an absolutely brilliant book. In his book, Matt has given us the insider's roadmap to follow in becoming powerful storytellers. As a business owner and entrepreneur for over five decades, I found this book to be full of pearls of wisdom and insight. If you speak to or communicate with people on any level, this book is a must-read."

—**DAVE ALBIN**, CEO, Founder, and Master Instructor at Firewalk Productions

"Winsome, vulnerable and practical, this page-turner calls us all to be intentional about what is often missing in business and life: the daring challenge to allow ourselves to be seen, even when this involves admitting that we've decorated an infant. Inspirational and entertaining. Don't miss it!"

—**JEFF LUCAS**, author, speaker, and broadcaster

"Nothing builds trust than a humble, engaging, and authentic story that speaks to the heart of you and your brand. This book will teach you to focus on winning the heart before winning the business."

—**JB KELLOGG**, CEO of Madwire

"Matt Shoup is the real deal. He has taken advantage of the opportunities he has been given, sometimes having massive success, sometimes having a 'learning experience.' Through his life and business experiences, he shares how he builds trust with his clients, and if you do the same, you will have not only raving fans but also friends for life."

—**DAVE SANDERSON**, President of Dave Sanderson Speaks International

PAINTED BABY

PAINTED
BABY

Connect with Clients Through

BRAVE AND VULNERABLE STORYTELLING

MATT SHOUP

LIONCREST
PUBLISHING

PAINTED BABY

Connect with Clients through Brave and Vulnerable Storytelling

ISBN		
	978-1-5445-3584-5	*Hardcover*
	978-1-5445-3582-1	*Paperback*
	978-1-5445-3583-8	*Ebook*

To you, my fellow entrepreneur, who's already taken a risk
by becoming a business owner and leader.

I am proud of you for taking this risk and believing in yourself.
I am inspired by your bravery. You truly are amazing!

In this book, I'll ask you to take another risk and step deeper into
that bravery. I believe in you and believe that you are up to the task.

You have a story. An important story, an impactful story,
a story that others need to hear.

I am excited and inspired to journey with you through
discovering this story and sharing it with others.

I hope this book inspires and encourages you to
take the next brave step toward excellence in your life,
your leadership, and your business.

I love you. You've got this. Together, let's go get it.

CONTENTS

INTRODUCTION

I've got a dirty little secret. So do you. We're actually going to talk about them in this book. Are you ready?

I'll go first.

In the spring of 2011, I was about to close the biggest business deal of my life. My residential painting company, M & E Painting, was still relatively new and landing this project would be a game-changer. But what happened to me that day was bigger than the painting project. What happened in that office changed my business and my relationships with my clients, my team, my vendors, and others close to me. It changed my life.

So, I was sitting across the desk from this guy, Bill. Like me, Bill had worked his way up from nothing. Unlike me, he had been an early shareholder in what became a very well-known company. Bill had started out sweeping floors, and then worked his way up in management, slowly investing in private stock in the business. When it went public, he had a very large payday. The money changed Bill's life, but it didn't change Bill. He was still a straight-shooting, hard-working, coffee-drinking, cigar-smoking guy.

So, what was a guy like me doing talking to a guy like this? Well, Bill was not just a client; he was a friend. I met him years ago and had done projects for him in the past, but nothing like this one. This proposal was for a massive custom staining project on Bill's second home, a place he called his million-dollar baby.

Right then, we were sitting in his primary residence, a Spanish-style mansion set on a golf course. This isn't the first time I had been in the place, but every time I visited it seemed bigger and more impressive. I walked through the iron gates, past his putting green, and across the courtyard with its fancy firepit and landscaping. I walked through the ten-foot-high, stained, solid wood front door and into Bill's office, reminding myself just how well he's done for himself, maybe better than I realized, and that this project—if I get it—could change my business. Not if I get it, but when I get it. Because Bill always signs the contract. And I always close the deal.

Before we got to my proposal—the potentially life-changing one I had so carefully prepared and tucked into a portfolio—we drank coffee and caught up on small talk. I hadn't seen Bill in a while, and we had a lot to catch up on. Bill looked comfortable, leaned back in his high-backed leather executive chair. We talked about what had been going on in our businesses and in our lives. After a while, Bill leaned in. It was time to talk business.

I'd had my company, M & E Painting, for five years at that point, and most projects were in the $4,000 range. The proposal I was setting on Bill's desk was for close to $60,000. It was a fair price for the work involved. And even though I'd known Bill a long time, and done work for him in the past, I still had to sell it. So, I did what I always did. I reminded him of how smoothly those other projects went, and I talked to him about my company's 98 percent client satisfaction rating. I went through the whole Sales 101 spiel: features, benefits, ask for the business, handle objections, and close the deal. That day, I used my "either or close," where I gave the client two options. It's a good close that worked almost every time. I pushed the contract across the desk along with a nice pen I brought just for this momentous occasion, and I asked Bill which option he'd like to go with.

This is where the client usually signs the contract. Bill, being the decisive guy he is, always signed it. With other clients, sometimes there were questions—what we in the sales world call "objections"— but like any great salesperson, I was prepared to handle those if they came up. Bill could have had questions this time. He may have wanted to negotiate. After all, this was a major deal. But I was prepared for the questions, the objections, the negotiations.

What I was not prepared for was what Bill did next.

He didn't pick up the pen. He didn't even look at the contract. Instead, he slid it back across the desk toward me, like he was rejecting it. Then he leaned back in that big chair, and I could tell by the look on his face that I missed something.

"Matt," he said, "I don't know if I'm ready to do this."

Okay, I thought, Bill has questions. Let the tennis match of objection-handling begin.

Bill said nothing, but my mind was going a mile a minute, trying to figure out what I missed. My sales wheels were spinning—*what objection haven't I handled?*

"Bill," I said, "I've always done great work for you, so what is it exactly that is preventing you from making this decision?" I could have said those words in my sleep; I've closed so many deals with them.

"Matt," he said, "sure, you've done great work in the past but this one's special. It's my million-dollar baby."

"Of course, I can see that, and I'm going to take good care of you," I said. I went back to my old spiel of the features, the benefits, and oh, by the way, have you seen our website lately and all the five-star reviews and the stellar Better Business Bureau rating?

I gently pushed the contract back toward Bill and resorted to my scarcity close.

"Well, Bill, you know we only have so many spots left. Your house is up in the mountains in Wyoming. It's going to get cold up there, and harder to do all the interior work without opening the windows. So, we should start soon. Let's get this on the books so we can move on it this year."

Bill looked at me, but...were his eyes starting to glaze over? I didn't think he was even listening anymore. It was time to break out my shiny marketing brochure, which of course I had tucked in the folder along with the contract, for just such occasions.

Bill flipped through the pages of my eight-page, three-dollars-and-twenty-five-cents brochure with its full-color photographs and all the right words to dazzle any client, close any deal.

Bill looked at the shiny marketing brochure. Then he looked at me. Then he picked up that shiny marketing brochure and tossed it across the room. It bounced off a bookcase and landed on the floor.

I sat up straight in my chair. *What just happened?*

Bill sat up in his chair and leaned across his desk, eyes focused on mine. "Your shiny marketing brochure is crap, Matt. I want to hear about something you screwed up and what you did about it. So, why don't you start there?"

What the heck? My mind was spinning. Everything I knew about sales and putting my best foot forward with my shiny brochure just got short-circuited. *And did Bill just raise his voice to me?*

Bill sat back, sipped his coffee, and waited for my response.

"You want to hear about a time when something didn't go well, is that what I heard you say?" I asked.

"That's what I said, Matt. I didn't stutter, did I?"

Okay, I've got this. I can do this. I have never done something like this before, but Bill asked for it, so here I go.

"Well, Bill, last year we had a very busy summer. There was one project where I picked up the paint and dropped it off at a house. My guys had the place all scraped and primed and ready to go. They painted the house and it all looked great until the homeowner showed up and told us it was the wrong color."

I waited for Bill's response. Now you need to understand that Bill's a Midwest transplant who wound up in Colorado, but somewhere along the way he picked up a bit of a Texas twang. Although he dressed very casually, normally wearing jeans or golf shorts and a T-shirt, I still sort of pictured him in my mind as wearing a ten-gallon hat and cowboy boots, chewing on a blade of grass.

"Whoa," he said, and I could hear that twang. "So, you painted the house the wrong color?"

"Yup," I said, with a shrug. "That was a bad day, but we made it right, of course. Got the right paint ordered and had the place repainted just a few days later."

"Well," said Bill, "I bet that happens with those guys down at the paint store all the time. They work with a lot of contractors, you know."

I nodded because he was right—they don't always get the paint right, but we usually check it before we start painting.

That's a good story, I thought, *so maybe now he'll sign the contract.*

"That's pretty bad, Matt, but it's not bad enough. Remember this is my million-dollar baby we're talking about." Bill leaned back, put his feet up on the corner of his desk, and grinned. "Try again. What's the *worst* thing that has happened?"

"Okay, well, painting the wrong color on the right house was pretty bad, Bill, but another time, we painted the right color on the wrong house. Do you want to hear about that?"

Bill sat up and leaned across his desk. "You did what? Of course, I want to hear about *that*. Do tell."

So, I told him about the time a few years back when...well, let me just tell you what happened.

About ten or fifteen years ago, I did all the sales and all the estimates for the business. I was managing the appointments too, ordering paint and getting it to my crew at the job sites. One morning, and just another day at the office, I called in an order and asked the gentleman at the paint store, Scott, to deliver it to 2710 Blue Sky Drive.

So, I headed out of the office to do an estimate when my phone rang. It was the crew lead, Brian, the foreman from my painting crew.

"Hey, Matt," he said, "we're ready to go here, but where's the paint?"

Now the paint should have been delivered, so I asked him to look around.

"Nope, no paint. We've been here all morning, Matt. We would have seen it."

"Okay," I told him, "I'll call the paint store and see what's going on. Just keep the crew busy there."

"There's nothing left to do," he said. "We got the whole place scraped, caulked all the seams and nail holes, masked the windows and the bushes. Even done spraying and brushing primer on the whole place. We're just waiting for the paint."

I called the paint store and they confirmed the paint was delivered an hour ago. So, I called Brian back.

"Hey, Brian, the paint store says they left in on the front porch next to the flowerpot."

"There's no paint on the front porch," he said. "There isn't even a flowerpot."

This wasn't making sense. I asked Brian if the guys had been drinking that morning or smoking a little of the funny stuff. I mean, how could they not see the paint?

"Alright, I'm coming there," I told him, thinking about how if I want something done right, I have to do it myself. On the way over, I called Scott at the paint store and let him have it. This was my business, and I was paying my guys to sit on their butts because there's no paint. By the time I got to the job site, I was fuming.

The weird thing is that when I pulled up to 2710 Blue Sky Drive, nobody was there. No ladders. No painters. No evidence of any work being done at all. I called Brian again.

"Hey," I told him, "where are you guys? You're supposed to be at the house!"

"Matt," he said, "we're here at 2710 Blue Sky Court. Where are you?"

I looked at the house. It was the right house, and I could even see the house number, *2710*. Then I looked at the street sign: *Blue Sky Drive*. This was definitely the right place. Then I realized what Brian just said: *2710 Blue Sky Court*.

I had sent my painting crew to the wrong house. And they had just scraped, caulked, masked, and primed the home of a family who never asked us to do so.

. . .

After telling Bill how badly I'd messed up, I told him what I did about it: how I waited for the homeowner, whom I had never met, so I could explain why his house was scraped and prepped for a paint project. (That homeowner was furious, by the way.) I told Bill how I had pleaded with him to see past the mistake and let my crew come back later, paint his house for free, and not sue me. I told him about how I dealt with the homeowner of the right house, who wanted to know why his house wasn't painted that day. And how I called Scott at the paint store to apologize for being such a big, massive jerk that morning.

So, there they were—my two worst stories. I'd painted the right house the wrong color, and I'd almost painted the right color on the wrong house. But as much as I had messed up, I'd taken responsibility and done what I could to make everything right too.

Now it was my turn to lean back. Bill *had* to sign the contract. I waited for his response. The proposal was still sitting between us, on his desk. My shiny marketing brochure was still on the floor. I had to wait for him to make the next move though. Sales 101: Know when to stop selling. Know when to stop *talking*.

Bill laughed and said, "Whoa, Matt—unbelievable! That's better than your first story."

"Yeah, I guess," I said, a little embarrassed, but relieved that he was laughing—and that he hadn't thrown me out of his office.

"Okay, then," I said, "can we do business now? Let's get your million-dollar baby on the schedule before it gets too cold. You know, they're calling for an early winter..."

"Not so fast, Matt," he said. "I feel like you're holding out on me. All these years in business? All those projects? You've got to have something better, and I'd love to hear it. Come on, what's the worst—I mean, absolute *worst*—you've ever done?"

By this point, I was wondering if Bill was messing with me. Or if he knew something about me that I didn't. But I looked at him and he was serious. So I racked my brain, trying to recall something bigger than the two stories I just told him.

"Matt," he said, "think about it. You've got something better. I know you do." He leaned back, put his feet on his desk, and took a sip of coffee like he had all day. Like he wasn't signing anything until he got what he wanted.

He had me and he knew it. My blood was about to boil and I could feel the color rising in my face.

"Okay, Bill, you got me," I said. "You really want to hear the *worst*?"

I didn't know what he was thinking now. Bill was ignoring me completely. He silently took another sip of his coffee.

It looked to me as if he had enough coffee in that cup to last him all morning, and there was no indication that he was going to let me leave his office until after I shared this story.

I took a deep breath.

"The worst thing I ever did," I said, "and I can't believe I'm telling you this, but the worst *we* ever did was…"

Bill was looking at me, not saying anything, but I had his attention.

I took another deep breath, and then I blurted it out. Those four words I never, ever thought I'd say again.

"We painted a baby!"

Bill leaned across his desk.

"You *what*?"

"We painted a baby," I said, "and I'll tell you the whole story, but if I do, will you sign the contract?"

Bill smirked and said, "I'm not making any promises, but I sure as heck have to hear this story."

I told Bill my Painted Baby Story—the worst story of my career—and I'll tell you about it in Chapter 1. First, I want you to know what that story meant to me. It was a turning point in my business, but until that moment with Bill, I had buried it, promising never to tell it to anybody for any reason. Telling it to Bill, and what I did with that story next, changed not only my business, but it changed my life.

. . .

Do you feel a pressure to present and paint a picture of perfection in your business? Do you always feel like you have to present yourself as the perfect, five-star, A+, shiny marketing brochure version of you and your business? While doing so, deep down, do you struggle with knowing that this shiny marketing brochure is tinged with imperfections, two-star, D+ experiences, customer interactions, and outcomes to business interactions and relationships?

Are you afraid to show the real, raw, imperfect version of yourself, fearing that you will be judged, seen as less of a successful leader and business owner, or that you will lose credibility with your clients, team members, and people you serve? Above and beyond that, do you fear that along with losing credibility, you will lose business, revenue, profit, and the fuel that feeds your family?

Do you ever feel disconnected from the people in your life and business? I'm not talking about random people who wander in and out of your life—the cashier at the grocery store or the server at the sports bar—but the people with whom you spend the most time. The people you rely on. Your team, your clients, your colleagues, your friends, and your family.

I had always been a good student of business, marketing, and sales. I followed the rules. *Put your best foot forward. Share your best stories, your proudest achievements, and your greatest successes. Show them your shiny marketing brochure.* But I was disconnected from many people, especially my clients, and I didn't know why. I thought they wanted the shiny marketing brochure and the success stories, and that's what I had been giving them for years. I was afraid to show the real and imperfect version of myself. In fact, I had become so good at putting not just my best but my perfect foot forward that I had completely ignored, buried, and forgotten about the imperfect parts of my life and how I operated as a business owner. I felt like at every turn, in every interaction, meeting, sales call, and human interaction, it was showtime, and the show I was putting on was the Shiny Marketing Brochure Matt Show.

What I observed that day over a cup of coffee with Bill flipped everything I thought I knew about business, communication, and building relationships in business on its head. I wasn't willing to be vulnerable and didn't understand how much of a crutch those stories had become. Some were the right stories told the wrong way. Others were the wrong stories or the easy stories. They told my clients absolutely nothing about me and my team. Those stories didn't show clients how we dealt with adversity and disaster. They didn't show how we could truly shine when it mattered.

SSSHHH YOUR DIRTY LITTLE SECRET

Your best worst story is the story you don't want to share with anyone. It's the story that flies in the face of your shiny marketing brochure; in fact, it could very well disprove and invalidate your shiny marketing brochure. It's the story that you fear could lose you business, crush your credibility, break down trust and connection in a relationship, and have another person judge you harshly and not do business with you. It's the story that you may be currently mortified to verbalize, write, or communicate in any way.

Your best worst story is your worst moment, your biggest embarrassment, your most massive screw up or letdown. Your super-duper, no good, horrible day in business. It's a time when you and your business showed up not at your best, but your worst. That story hides within you, safe from the world. It is locked and you have thrown away the key, keeping this story highly guarded, protected, possibly so well that you have even forgotten about or deny its very existence.

Yet, your best worst story is your most powerful tool to building deeper connections. I call that best worst story (or dirty little secret) the Painted Baby Story, or "PBS" for short.

Bill had forced me into a moment of vulnerability. I needed him to sign that contract. My reluctance and fear-filled giving in to that vulnerability unlocked a part of me that I had never shared with my clients, my team members, or many other people in my life. Unlocking that part of me, that authentic and true part of me that wasn't perfect, opened the door to connection and trust. I just needed to walk through it.

CONNECTION THROUGH STORY

I started my painting business almost twenty years ago. Hungry and motivated to build my company as quickly as possible, I took on as many projects as I could manage. *Work harder and work more* was my motto. I wasn't focused on efficiency. I didn't think about getting bigger projects for less effort or creating connections that drove repeat business. My business grew, but it didn't scale, and I was burning out.

Every entrepreneur I know has days when they ask themselves, "Why am I doing this? Is it even worth it?" Those days pass, and the next day is better, and we press on. That day in Bill's home, I was at one of those low points and needed to turn it around quickly.

Bill's initial refusal to sign the contract—despite all my best efforts—was a wake-up call. You see, I was doing my best to play the part of a confident, successful business owner, but the truth is, I was tired. The stress of fighting for every proposal, every project, was getting to me. The long hours spent dealing with my team, with the paint store, and with clients, were killing me. Most days, surrounded by people, I felt completely alone. I still loved my business, but it wasn't loving me back, and I wanted more time for myself and for the people who did love me—my family and friends.

In my mind, I was already considering hanging it up, but Bill's million-dollar baby project was so big that landing it, I figured, might be enough to keep me hanging on. I didn't expect what happened that day and could never have predicted the impact it would have on my business. Getting called out changed everything. Bill's challenge to tell my Painted Baby Story (PBS) opened the door to a different way of doing business that I didn't know existed.

What I observed that day was counterintuitive. It went against everything I thought I knew about business, sales, marketing, leadership, and ultimately, life. By telling Bill my story, and by him hearing it, we connected on a different level. That conversation taught me that how much and how well I was willing and able to connect with people on a deeper level determined my success. But connecting, I learned, took vulnerability. It took putting myself out there in a way I never had. This was a language I did not speak, nor understand.

Putting myself out there had nothing to do with putting on an air of confidence, telling my success stories, or using clever closes to get the business. And it had absolutely nothing to do with my shiny marketing brochure. Connecting with people and earning their trust started with giving of myself, my real self. I had to let down my guard and show them who I was, and the way to do that was with a story. Not just any story, but a story I never thought I'd tell anyone. My best worst story. My Painted Baby Story.

First let me tell you what brought me to writing this book.

STOP! HIT THE BRAKES

We all have a shiny marketing brochure that we show the world. It may be a different brochure for our families, our friends, our team, and our clients. Think about your own shiny marketing brochure. What does it look like? What is included in the stories you tell? For now, jot down some of your thoughts. We'll address these later in the book.

By the way, you'll see these "Stop! Hit the Brakes" boxes throughout the book. These are tiny actions that will ease you into brave and vulnerable storytelling. I encourage you to pause this book and follow the instructions when you see these boxes.

WHY I WROTE THIS BOOK

Have you ever had an epiphany, a moment of clarity, or a life-changing lesson? In doing so, were you inspired to share it with those you care about, those you are responsible to serve, the ones you love?

When I had my Painted Baby moment and realized what had come from it and how it changed my business, I could not keep it to myself. I love business; I love people. I love helping business owners grow, have a better life, enhance and develop their leadership, to own and live their lives, their stories, their businesses with excellence.

I wrote this book to give you a strategy to leverage your and your company's worst moments and use them as a deliverable story, creating growth opportunities for your company. These growth opportunities involve deeper connection with people, and more business coming your way. I wrote this book to challenge you to consider and test the hypothesis I tested after telling Bill my Painted Baby Story. That hypothesis is:

Being real, vulnerable, and 100 percent honest in business builds deeper trust and connection with clients and those you serve, and this is what ultimately grows your business.

I wrote this book for business owners and leaders who are missing out on that most critical piece of all in their business: the people, and connecting with them at a true, deep, meaningful level.

This book is meant to challenge, encourage, and inspire you to come clean about who you are and what you've done. The good, the bad, the ugly. Storytelling makes it a lot easier though. I am going to step you through the exact process that I went through to explore, develop, and share your story, your Painted Baby Story. I will also give you my best advice on how you can use what I observed through this process to make dramatic improvements to your business.

Reflecting back on my years as a business owner, I have observed many instances where I missed opportunities to establish and build deeper and more meaningful relationships due to my own inability to recognize that a process existed and how the process actually worked. This book is meant to inspire you to uncover and discover the power of your story and leverage it to build deeper trust and connection with others, which will in turn grow your business.

You might think I'm crazy. A lot of people thought I was crazy when I started telling my Painted Baby Story. I proved them wrong, and I want you to prove people wrong too by telling your Painted Baby Story. We'll prove them wrong together, you and I, because we're both better than a shiny marketing brochure and all the success stories that make us look really good but can hide our more imperfect side. We have to be brave enough to uncover that other side if we want to become better business owners, leaders, and people.

We deserve more, our people deserve more, and our clients deserve more too. Heck, our families deserve a lot more, but we can't give that to them until we come clean and embrace all the not-so-perfect parts of ourselves.

You may have picked up this book because the cover grabbed your attention, or you were intrigued by the title. Maybe you're looking for a way to connect with your clients, but you don't know where to start. Clients are people—they are among the many people who you connect with in your business and on a day-to-day basis. While this book is client-focused, you will see that the lessons found in my story and in the stories of other business owners that I share in this book are true for client relationships, but they are just as true for building deeper connections with other people who touch your business.

I climbed a quick mountain of success with M & E Painting. When I got to the top of that mountain, I thought I was at the top of my career and my life. I carried along like that for a while, feeling good about myself but also knowing that something was missing. As it turned out, *I* was missing. I wasn't putting myself, my whole true self, into my business. When I did, everything changed. And it all started with the Painted Baby Story.

I am honored and looking forward to taking this journey with you. I am excited to share the stories of many other entrepreneurs who have decided to take this journey and share their Painted Baby Stories. I am honored to serve you, encourage you, inspire you, and challenge and push you to be better, in your business, your leadership, and your life.

Let's do this!

PART ONE

THE POWER OF STORY

Before we continue, I want to let you know about the journey we are about to embark on together.

In Chapter 1, I will share my Painted Baby Story (PBS) exactly how I first shared it with Bill. From there, we will explore in Chapter 2 if you need to consider changing your story through a framework called the Three C's of Changing Your Story. Chapter 2 will challenge you to consider and evaluate how we connect as humans and how you may be missing an opportunity to connect with people, just as I was when this journey began. In Chapter 3, we will cover how to explore your story and begin to uncover and discover the powerful pieces of it so that you can begin to share them with the people you serve. We will also address why many people fear and do not commit to sharing their story. In Chapter 4, we'll return to the PBS and a hypothesis that I developed around when, where, and why to share your PBS. I tested my hypothesis, and you'll see the results in Chapter 4. In Chapter 5, the final chapter of Part One, I will share what I did once I saw these results and how I took this message to a greater audience in my business market, which created a massive uptick in business.

CHAPTER 1

THE PAINTED BABY STORY

"I bet this one's going to be good."

Bill was waiting for my story. My best worst story. My Painted Baby Story.

"I guess," I said. I had never told this story to anyone. To me, it was a dirty secret, something I never wanted my competition—or anyone else—to know. As I prepared to share it with Bill, I felt like pinching myself. *Am I in a dream? This is the biggest deal of my life, and I could be blowing it.*

"All right, Bill. Here you go."

. . .

Before I can fully explain the PBS, allow me to set the scene a bit.

I live in Northern Colorado, about one hour north of Denver and twenty minutes south of Fort Collins in the city of Loveland. By 2008, M & E Painting, named for myself and my wife, Emily, was well established and thriving in both Loveland and Fort Collins.

One typical, sunny Colorado day in May, clouds began to fill the sky and weather forecasters issued a warning that a tornado was set to land in the nearby town of Windsor. Tornadoes were known to ravage the plains in Eastern Colorado, but they were practically unheard of in this part of the state due to our proximity to the Rocky

Mountains. As predicted, just before noon a three-quarter-mile-wide tornado touched down, journeyed for 39 miles, and ripped through and ravaged the town of Windsor, causing one death and dozens of injuries. The tornado also caused catastrophic damage to some residential neighborhoods. Many homes were hit with tens to hundreds of thousands of dollars' worth of damage. Some homes were completely destroyed and leveled.

I felt awful for the people of Windsor, and I also knew they would be looking desperately for contractors to help get their homes back in shape. My paint crews and I headed to the area, where we teamed up with roofers and construction companies to let people know we were there to help them with their home reconstruction needs. Together, we lined up dozens of contracts with nine of them being on one street in the popular Water Valley subdivision.

Two of our painters, brothers Blas and Raul, worked on those nine houses. Typically, it took them three days to prepare a house for painting, spray the main portions of the house, and then paint the trim and doors. One house belonged to a small family: a busy, working man, his wife, and their nine-month-old daughter. Mrs. Angelo was particularly kind and friendly. You could tell that she absolutely loved people, including me and my crew. She left a cooler full of drinks and snacks on her front porch for us while we worked, and she often came out to chat and see how we were doing.

At this point in my business, I hadn't mastered the art of delegation. I was still out selling projects, doing bank deposits, and managing just about everything else outside of actually painting the homes. My wife, Emily, took care of fielding phone calls in the home office and managing the accounting for the business.

On a Tuesday afternoon, I was on my way to the bank and then off to a meeting with a potential client. As I walked into the bank, my phone rang. The display read *Raul*. I silenced the phone, setting it to vibrate, and planned to call him back as soon as I left the bank. Four seconds later, my phone buzzed. Again, it was Raul. A few seconds later, another call. Annoyed, I muted the phone completely and shoved it in my pocket.

The next time I looked at my phone, there were eight missed calls. I quickly phoned Raul.

When he answered, he began screaming incoherently. I could not make out most of what he was yelling, but I did hear him say:

"Matteo, Matteo, come quick!"

A bit of background on Raul: Spanish is his first language, and English, his second. English is my first language and Spanish, my second. Working together, we spoke to each other in Spanglish, a mixture of both. Raul is also a BIG jokester, the class clown of M & E Painting. He was always pranking me, calling to insist I come quickly to a job site to resolve spilled paint, a dropped ladder, or some other fabricated disaster.

This call was different. His voice was different. It was hard to distinguish what he was screaming at me in Spanish as I also heard Blas screaming in the background. I then heard a woman talking and a baby crying loudly. Wailing.

"Raul, *¿qué pasó?*" I asked. *What's going on?*

"Matteo," he says. "You have to come quick! Just get here now. *The paint and the gun and the boom and the baby.* Matteo, Matteo, come quick!" His words barely made sense.

Then, "Matteo, *I PAINT THE BABY!*"

"What?" I screamed.

"I PAINT THE BABY," he cried. "Matteo, come quick." Then he hung up.

I was twenty minutes away from his location in Windsor, standing in front of the bank, stunned. I jumped in my car and raced to the job site.

When I arrived, Raul's brother, Blas, was in the street, next to his truck, attempting to clean drop sheets, buckets, hand tools, and T-shirts that were soaked with black paint.

I rushed to him, yelling, "Blas, what's happening?"

"Man, no lo sé. *I don't know.* You need to see Raul." He didn't want to tell me what had happened.

Walking up to the house, I saw black paint dripping down the driveway. In the backyard, a huge explosion of paint was splattered all over the house, the landscaping, the barbecue grill, the concrete patio, the flagstone walkway, the perimeter fence, and all over Blas and Raul.

Raul stood there, eyes wide, and a spray gun at his feet. I felt like I had walked into a crime scene, but instead of blood, the perpetrator had splattered, sprayed, and exploded paint everywhere. All around, I could see what looked like an attempt to clean up the mess of paint. Mrs. Angelo was nowhere in sight.

"What happened?" I roared. It's not like me to yell at my crew, but I couldn't believe what I was seeing, and my emotions got the best of me.

Raul explained. He and Blas had shown up on time to paint the house and as usual, Mrs. Angelo had come out to greet them and left them some snacks and drinks. She continued to pop in on the crew to see how they were doing throughout the morning—and, each time, she was holding her nine-month-old baby girl. Mrs. Angelo commented on how well the project was coming along. They got to work, and throughout the morning, Mrs. Angelo had come outside to admire their progress. Around noon, she gave them sodas and sandwiches, and after they ate, the men got back to work.

Most of the project was done, but there was still the service door to the garage to paint. Raul readied the spray gun, while Mrs. Angelo stood behind him, still holding her baby daughter.

"I should have warned her to stand back," he said, "but I guess I wasn't thinking. I just picked up the gun and aimed it at the door."

Paint sprayers are high-pressure, piston-driven machines that take paint from the bucket, through a hose, and out of a spray gun, applying the paint in a nice, consistent, and evenly controlled spray pattern onto the surface. What Raul didn't know was that the spray tip within the spray gun had somehow become slightly misaligned and jammed within the gun. When he pulled the trigger, the highly pressurized black paint exploded everywhere. It splattered everywhere, and in its path, were Raul, Blas, Mrs. Angelo, and...

HER BABY! Her nine-month-old baby girl!

I was probably in shock for a minute. I couldn't believe my ears. But I had to check in on the Angelos, and I did. Those few short minutes walking up to the front door to check in on the Angelos felt like an eternity. My heart was pounding a million miles a minute. I was visibly shaking, and I was sweating profusely.

Mrs. Angelo opened the door and greeted me with a smile. *A smile*, I thought, *how can you be smiling after you and your baby were just attacked by a paint sprayer?* Thankfully and luckily, they were alright. Mrs. Angelo had bathed the baby, and there was no harm done. She did have to throw away all of her clothes and the baby's clothes too.

I breathed a huge sigh of relief, knowing that the outcome could have been so much worse. I couldn't help but go through every "what if" scenario in my mind. What if Mrs. Angelo had been standing even closer? What if the paint explosion caused her to drop her baby? The terror of knowing that my business could have caused someone harm—caused a *small child* harm—was sickening. I got a cold chill thinking about it, realizing how lucky we had been.

. . .

"I've never told that story, Bill. It was my worst day in the business and actually, one of the worst days of my life. I still feel horrible about it."

Bill just stared at me. I was nervous, shaky. I needed him to say something.

"Bill, what do you want from me? I don't have anything else."

He leaned forward in his seat, eyes wide. "Well, what did you *do*, Matt?"

"Like I said, I made sure everyone was alright. I mean, I couldn't even imagine how traumatic this was for Mrs. Angelo and her daughter. Then I checked in on Raul and Blas to make sure they were okay too. They weren't injured, but they were really shaken up. I mean, think about it. They were worried about Mrs. Angelo of course, but they were also worried about the project."

Bill nodded his head.

"And they were worried about their *jobs* too. This was a disaster that no one saw coming and here I was, the boss, just showing up for the aftermath. Of course, I was freaked out, but I understood that it was an accident. This wasn't the time to be pointing fingers and blaming people. This was my team and we had to work together to take care of the mess. There was paint to clean up and we still had a project to finish."

Telling my Painted Baby Story, I observed that Bill was absolutely intrigued. Not only intrigued but fully engaged. Earlier in the conversation, he was barely interested in what I had said. He seemed to ignore me as the broken record of "Matt the amazing salesman song" played on and on. But after hearing the story, he leaned in, hanging on every word. He didn't look at me like this when I told him about my five-star, A-plus, shiny marketing brochure.

He wanted to know what comes next. The more details I shared about my horror story, the more he wanted to hear. I was like the car wreck on the side of the road that everyone slows down to leer at but no one wants to be a part of.

I talked Bill through the rest of the disaster. I explained to him how we cleaned up the house and reimbursed Mrs. Angelo $437 to pay for all the ruined clothes and a new onesie for the baby. I explained to him about how we replaced the ruined flagstone and spent countless hours scrubbing black paint off everything within a forty-foot radius of the exploded paint gun. I told him that we eventually restored everything, painted the house, sent the Angelos out to a very nice dinner, and closed out the project with very happy clients.

"The Angelos forgave us. They knew it was an accident and appreciated that we owned up to it and did everything we could to make it right."

Upon one of our final conversations, Mrs. Angelo made sure that the painters and I fully understood that she and her husband were not angry or upset, and that they did not hold any hard feelings toward us. We actually had a final laugh about the story before parting ways.

Despite the happy ending, when it was all over, I parked that story in the deepest recesses of my mind. Just revisiting it, telling Bill about it, brought a shiver to my spine. I was glad it was over, and I had resolved to never talk about it again.

But right then, I looked at Bill and took in his reaction. He attentively listened to the whole story and for the last five minutes, I saw all his emotions: shock, curiosity, laughter, and disbelief. Bill was pulled into the story, and he wanted to hear more of the dramatic details at every turn.

"Whelp, there you go," I said, resigned to the fact that I just killed any chances of getting any more business from my old friend Bill. "That's what you wanted; that's what you got." I didn't cry, but I kind of wanted to. I wanted to run out of that place before Bill threw me out. *I wonder which door*, I thought, *the front door? Back door? Is there a side door to this place?* My brain was short-circuiting and I was waiting for Bill to stop laughing and pick a door. *Wait, he's laughing?*

Bill sat up straight and looked me straight in the eye. *Here it comes.*

"That's the worst thing that's gone wrong? Your biggest screw-up? And you handled it?" he said.

"Yeah, it is," I replied.

Bill extended his hand for me to shake it, and then he said something to me—the last thing I expected him to say.

"Okay, then, Matt, give me that paper and let's get this done." Stunned, I handed Bill the contract. He signed it and pushed it back across the desk. *The $60,000 contract. The biggest deal of my career.* The shock was clear on my face. For the first time in my life, I was speechless.

"Matt, if that's the worst day of business that you've had and that's how you dealt with it, I can envision all the worst-case scenarios with this project. And now I know that no matter how well the project goes or if something bad happens, I can count on you to stand by your work and your people," he explained. "I trust you, and you're the kind of guy I want to do business with."

So, that was it. I got it. I couldn't believe it, but I got it. I was sort of in a state of shock as I shook Bill's hand, mumbled a thank-you and good-bye, and gathered up the paperwork, and the shiny marketing brochure, which I tucked away into a folder, embarrassed that I even brought it out in the first place. I was still stunned as I walked out of Bill's million-dollar house, through his Spanish court-yard, past his putting green, and through the gate. In my pocket, I had a huge check—a 50 percent deposit on the biggest contract I'd ever landed.

My head was spinning. The meeting with Bill went against every-thing I had ever been taught about sales and business and working and connecting with clients. *This is not how you close the biggest deal of your career.*

I had just shared my deepest, darkest, dirtiest business secret—a secret I had promised myself to never share again. Instead of ruin-ing any chances of closing the deal, telling my PBS had the opposite effect. For once in my life, I had stopped playing the business owner, the sales guy, the closer—and gotten real with somebody. I had con-nected with another human being in a way I never had before. And not just in my painting business, but in my entire life. I never wanted people to know about my shortcomings, imperfections, or traumas. I tried to hide them, to airbrush over them. My whole life, I was play-ing the role of the shiny marketing brochure, never realizing that the slick pages—my slick exterior—wasn't drawing people in. It was sep-arating us and preventing us from true connection.

THE AFTERMATH

I had a whiteboard in my sales office where our salespeople logged their deals for the week, so we could see how business was shaping up. Putting those numbers up for all to see served as motivation to pursue our goals, while creating a bit of competition among us. Coming back to the office after my meeting with Bill, I checked out the board: Nick had closed $12,000 for the week and TJ had closed $15,000—good numbers. My hand shook as I carefully wrote my number for the day—$60,000.

TJ, one of my best salespeople, looked at me and said, "Woah, Matt. What the heck are we painting?"

"You're not going to believe it," I replied. "I just landed the big stain project with Bill."

"Awesome! Did you hit him with the over-under close or the takeaway close?"

Everyone in the room stared at me, curious about the particular "close" I'd used to bring in this massive deal.

"I used all of them. Every close in the book."

I could see that everybody was smiling, until I followed up with, "And none of them worked."

"What do you mean?" said TJ. "How the heck did you close the deal then?"

"Um, well...I told Bill about the time we painted the baby."

"You did *what*?"

Everyone stood there with their mouths open. They knew the story. I knew the story. They just couldn't believe I'd tell anyone else about what happened that day in Mrs. Angelo's backyard.

Then I told them the whole story about my meeting with Bill. I told them about his million-dollar baby, my pitch, the shiny marketing brochure (and what Bill did with it). I told them about giving Bill the "painting-the-right-house-the-wrong-color" story and the "painting-the-wrong-house-the-right-color" story. And how Bill wasn't impressed.

"I knew that telling the Painted Baby Story was a Hail Mary, but it was all I had left," I said. "And it worked."

The whole team was speechless, like I was when Bill signed the contract. I had to think about what happened. I needed time to figure it out and give my team a better answer than, "I don't know what happened and I don't know why it happened." They wanted to know. *I* wanted to know.

This was not how business is supposed to work.

MY HYPOTHESIS

My original hypothesis was, "Share PBS, close more business." That was a surface-level-sales-based hypothesis. Later, I realized that hypothesis was all wrong because I was still very much in sales mode instead of servant mode. My servant-based hypothesis, and the true lesson, was different.

Here is the hypothesis I proposed stemming from the sharing of my Painted Baby Story:

The hypothesis comprises three key concepts: 1) painting a picture of perfection prevents true connection; 2) sharing your Painted Baby Story allows you to become real, vulnerable and 100 percent honest with clients, thus entering into deeper conversations; and 3) being real, vulnerable, and 100 percent honest builds deeper trust and connection with clients and those you serve, and this is what ultimately grows your business.

Bill signed the contract, and that made me question everything I'd been doing. It changed how I interacted with people. It changed my relationships with my clients and my team. Telling my PBS set me on a journey that changed me.

HUMAN NEED FOR CONNECTION

I thought hard about what happened between Bill and me that day. Against my best judgment, I had let down my guard, made myself vulnerable, and told Bill a secret that I believed would destroy any chances of getting any more business from him. I had shared my worst train wreck with brutal honesty and offered him a front-row seat into the details. He got to see the worst of it without actually being involved in it. I pondered whether this is what people want from each other. Is this kind of raw honesty really necessary?

Sitting at my desk, my mind wandered to—of all places—Starbucks. A week or so earlier, I had been sitting in Starbucks with my laptop open, working while trying to drown out other's conversations, but I couldn't help but pick up bits and pieces of chatter. To my left, two men were talking about their businesses. My ears perked up—maybe I could glean some useful tidbits. The men went on and on about business projections, KPIs, and how their third quarter was shaping up. *Boring*, I thought, as I mentally turned down the volume on that conversation.

To my right, a young woman was recounting a bad dating experience to her male friend. She had met a guy on a dating app. He seemed to be exactly the kind of man she was looking for, or at least worthy of a first date. When he showed up in an old, beaten-up car, she reasoned that he was probably just frugal and didn't like spending money on fancy vehicles. She also felt a pang of guilt—who was she to be judging a guy by his choice of car? At least he wasn't saddled with a huge car payment!

Then the passenger side door opened, and a young man jumped out—her date. He escorted her to the car and pushed the front seat up so she could climb into the back. Up front, in the driver's seat, sat his mother. It was her old beater car, not his, and she was their driver for the night.

As I sat there, pretending to work in the Starbucks, I was drawn in by the drama of this young woman's story. She shared train wreck after train wreck, and I was captivated.

I observed that as humans, we're connected to drama. (Side note: I also observed that I like to eavesdrop on conversations at Starbucks. Is it just me?) We want to hear about crazy experiences and what comes out of them. It's not necessarily that we wish ill on other people, but rather that we want to hear how they handle difficult situations. We want to hear them be faced with a challenge, obstacle, or downright dramatic situation and hear how they reacted, responded, overcame, and persevered.

I also observed, listening to that conversation, that through storytelling we connect as humans. More importantly, that humans desire and yearn for connection. Maslow's Hierarchy of Needs explains human needs and the order in which we need them. At the bottom of his hierarchy are the very basic human needs: air, water, food, shelter, and sleep. Above those are security and safety needs. Just above those lie the human need to connect with others, forming bonds and relationships.

Thirdly, I observed that when one person opens the door of their lives that exposes a not-so-perfect side of themselves, the other person in the conversation reciprocates, taking this relationship to a new and different level of connection.

Let me ask you a question regarding the following stories. I will present to you *four* different people, each with two different stories they have to share with you. Imagine each one of these stories is sitting on either side of you at the local coffee shop. Which one catches more of your attention? Which one do you lean into more? Which one gives you the opportunity to learn more about who these people are, what they stand for, and paves the way for a deeper connection.

DAVE SANDERSON

Dave S's Story #1: Meet Dave Sanderson with Dave Sanderson Speaks. I met Dave at an Entrepreneur's Organization event in Atlantic City, New Jersey, in 2013. We were both speakers at this event. Dave spent years as a high-level sales executive with a large software company. He spent many days on the road traveling to close business deals. Dave was a buttoned-up, well-spoken, highly driven, and successful salesperson.

Dave S's Story #2: On January 15th, 2009, US Airways Flight 1549 took off from LaGuardia airport in New York. This was supposed to be a routine, fairly short flight down to South Carolina that Dave had taken many times. Shortly after takeoff, the plane collided with a flock of birds, which in turn, took out both of the plane's engines. Dave, a passenger on the plane, took action that saved countless lives that day.

Which story would you prefer to hear?

DAVE ALBIN

Dave A's Story #1: I met Dave Albin, owner of Firewalk Adventures, through Dave Sanderson in 2014. Dave's company performs life-changing experiences for small business owners, entrepreneurs, and corporations around the world. He has hosted fire walks, glass walks, board breaks, and other transformational activities for thousands of people with companies such as Google, Chick-fil-A, NASA, Entrepreneurs Organization, and Heineken.

Dave A's Story #2: When Dave woke up the morning of June 8th, 1988, he was grossly addicted to alcohol and drugs. He had come to a point in his life where living with the devastating emotional and physical pain associated with these addictions needed to end. So, to end it, Dave went to his bedroom, loaded a pistol, and put it in his mouth.

Which story would you prefer to hear?

RICK SCADDEN

Rick's Story #1: Meet Rick Scadden, pastor at Citipointe Church in Loveland, Colorado. I met Rick in 2013 when he began working for M & E Painting. Rick loves the work he does to serve God, his community, and his church. He has a beautiful wife and three children, and he enjoys fishing, traveling, and spending time with his family.

Rick's Story #2: Before Rick was a full-time pastor, he was a four-time felon. He made a decision on July 4, 2004, that ultimately changed his life and the lives of many others.

Which story would you prefer to hear?

REALLY COOL CONTRACTOR

Really Cool Contractor's Story #1: Really Cool Contractor is a successful contractor in Northern Colorado. He's a personable guy and a rockstar at his job. I met Really Cool Contractor in 2019 at a local networking event and was immediately drawn in by his energy and personality. It seems, everywhere you go, Really Cool Contractor is there, and he is there doing business.

Really Cool Contractor's Story #2: Eight years ago, Really Cool Contractor was homeless, living under a bridge in Southern Florida selling water bottles. He had just moved out of a halfway house and was trying to build a better life. Every day was a struggle to survive for Really Cool Contractor, and one morning, he made a brave decision that would ultimately change his life and the direction of it.

Which story would you prefer to hear?

I'm guessing you chose the second story in each case. Don't feel bad about that—it's not like we enjoy other people's pain, and I am not here to exploit it. When someone shares their pain and struggle with us, we have to respect their bravery and vulnerability. They are opening the door to connect more with us and for us to share something back and connect with them about our own life experience and perspective. That is how deeper relationships are built.

When I shared my Painted Baby Story with Bill, he wanted to

know what would happen if my train wreck became his train wreck. He wanted to know how I would triage the chaos. He wanted the opportunity to connect more with me, and through me sharing this story with him, we did connect and connected at a deeper level.

What Bill saw in my story, which I had yet to see, was the integrity that I had as a business owner. I had previously thought my integrity came from my success stories, but it really came from me stepping up to own a not-so-perfect moment. He had already seen me at my best, but he wanted to see me at my worst too.

I put a lot of thought into what had happened that day, which established the hypothesis I shared with you. The following week, I presented it to my team at our leadership meeting. Something had changed between Bill and I when I told him my PBS. I thought back on his words: "I trust you, and you're the kind of guy I want to do business with."

Eventually, I shared my hypothesis with my team. I tested it in the field too and tracked the results. This new knowledge sparked what would become a whole new framework for how I interacted with clients. My new understanding of relationships and trust was a turning point for my business. I began working differently—not only with my clients, but with my company team members, vendors, and partners. Telling my Painted Baby Story changed my relationships with my clients and my team, and it also changed my relationships with people in my personal life. At work, I wasn't shiny marketing brochure Matt anymore. I wasn't clever-sales-close Matt. I became me—a regular guy who makes mistakes and is okay sharing them. More importantly, in business and in life, a guy who respects himself enough to tell the whole truth. A guy who cares about other people and has the integrity to correct his mistakes, especially when they impact those people. A guy who values honesty and realizes that life and work aren't about manipulating other people to control an outcome. It's about being real and accepting the results—and that if I didn't like those results, instead of trying to change what other people thought of me, I had to change myself.

JOIN IN THE JOURNEY

So, there you have it. You now know my PBS. As you read through it, I hope it did a couple of important things for you. First, I hope it made you laugh. Couldn't we all use a little more laughter in our lives and business? I hope it built a deeper connection between us and that you feel that you know me just a little more than you did when you picked up this book and began to read it.

I hope it also challenged your thinking, specifically, your thinking regarding how humans connect and engage, and how you are connecting and engaging with those in your business that you serve. I hope it challenged you to consider how you are communicating with and building relationships with your clients. I hope you consider the hypothesis I presented, and I hope you are ready to continue this journey with me through this book, where I will share how I tested it and what the results ended up being. I have much more to tell you about what I did with my story and how my business changed and improved, and how you can do the same with your stories changing and improving your business along the way.

I wouldn't have told these stories if Bill hadn't called me out that day in his office. He challenged me to own and share my Painted Baby Story, and now I'm challenging you to do the same.

DOWNLOAD MY FREE BUSINESS AND LEADERSHIP TOOLS

Throughout this book, we will conclude each chapter with some questions to consider. These questions are the foundation of the Painted Baby workbook. This workbook will help you to discover, build, and share your Painted Baby Story. Be sure to visit the link below and sign up for my free tools. I will send you the Painted Baby workbook along with many other free tools to help you build your business and advance your leadership.

→ https://www.mattshoup.com/free-tools/

QUESTIONS TO CONSIDER

Questions to Consider appear at the end of each chapter. Unlike the "Stop! Hit the Brakes" boxes, which I encourage you to act on as they appear, the questions take more time and more thought. Work through them at your own pace and return to them as you work through the corresponding concepts in their respective chapters. These questions can also be found in the Painted Baby workbook.

1. We've all made mistakes in business and in life. What are some of your best worst stories—your potential Painted Baby Stories? Jot them down for now; we'll talk about them more in the coming chapters.

2. Think about your current marketing and sales messaging. How are you communicating with your clients, your team,

and those around you with whom you do business? How much are you referring to or attempting to show only your shiny marketing brochure?

3. How do those around you respond to the way you are currently communicating with them?

4. Have you been vulnerable with any of the people in your business (your clients, your team, your vendors)? If so, how did they respond? What was the outcome?

5. How do you currently feel about opening up and being more vulnerable with the people you serve in business?

CHAPTER 2

DO YOU NEED TO CHANGE YOUR STORY?

Once a year, I host a leadership retreat for the members of my companies. We unplug from the day-to-day operations and spend a few days working on the business and on ourselves.

I keep my own speeches to a minimum during these retreats and instead invite guest speakers who can bring a fresh perspective to the team. As part of this retreat in December 2021, my great friend and former team member, Rick Scadden, who worked for M & E Painting from 2013–2019, addressed the group. Since leaving M & E Painting, Rick had become a full-time pastor. But a decade prior, Rick was a four-time felon.

A little background on Rick: He had started out doing work for M & E as an independent contractor. Rick initially caught my attention due to his amazing work ethic, skill set, and reliability and dependability. Pretty soon into our relationship, Rick's passion for and love of Jesus became very apparent. Rick quoted the Bible often and his life seemed to focus around following and serving Jesus and sharing the good word. He was what some might call a "Jesus freak." But every once in a while, his language and style of communicating changed. His soft, kind, Jesus-focused demeanor and biblical references temporarily shifted to aggressive outbursts, vengeful comments, and a complete change in his body language, manner of speech, and approach toward a situation that significantly caught my attention. The best way I would describe these moments is by saying that Rick went a little "sideways" for a minute. When this happened, I thought to myself, "What is this guy's story?"

In 2013, a leadership position opened at M & E and Rick expressed interest. He was one of our best contractors—reliable, positive, and engaging. On top of great work, he was well-liked by clients. If Rick wanted to put down the paintbrush and handsaw and take on a management position, it made sense to consider him for the position.

The next day I caught up with Rick to talk to him about the direction of the company. I wanted him to know what he was getting into and see if he was still interested. His interest didn't wane—in fact, he was totally onboard. But he had something to tell me first before I made up my mind to hire him into the business.

"Before we talk further, Matt, I have to be upfront with you," he said.

"*Matt*," he said, and there it was! He went sideways again and then told me, "Listen. I've got felonies, bro." The way he spoke those words reflected the same demeanor and tone that would pop up from time to time during those aggressive outbursts.

That got my attention, but I didn't take his words seriously. I thought he was half joking for a minute. I kind of laughed and said, "What do you mean you have felonies? Did you not pay some parking tickets? There is no way you are telling me the truth."

Rick wasn't laughing. Rick wasn't joking. Rick was 100 percent serious, and I saw that seriousness in his face. He then asked permission to share a story. His story. This is a story I will never forget. He shared with me his PBS.

• • •

Rick grew up in a rough neighborhood just north of Denver, Colorado, that was rife with drug addicts and the crime associated with people whose lives revolve around doing drugs and breaking the law to pay for them. His earliest memory was of his mom and himself being kidnapped at gunpoint, and while he remembered the shotgun being pointed at his mom's head, he doesn't remember why they were kidnapped or how they got away. Rick's father was in and out of jail, so he didn't have a male role model during most of his childhood. He started drinking, smoking pot, and doing cocaine before he was a teenager.

Rick met a girl, and they were engaged, but his lifestyle didn't change. He was still partying all the time. One Fourth of July evening, Rick and his friends were gathered for a party. After a day of hard drinking and partying, he learned that his fiancé was cheating on him. Not only did he find out at the party, but he also found out the man she was cheating on him with was at the party. Rick was furious; jumping into his pickup truck in a drunken rage, he sped away from the party. Racing and ripping through town, he blew through three red lights, and on the fourth one, he T-boned another vehicle. He was going sixty-five miles an hour.

Rick was knocked out momentarily from the impact. When he woke up, he was greeted by a police officer and EMT who asked what happened. Rick had no memory of what had just occurred. His drugs, shotguns, ammunition, and stacks of cash had flown from the truck and littered the intersection. He passed out again.

The next time he woke up, he was handcuffed to a hospital bed. A police officer told him he was being charged with vehicular assault. Another officer asked him about the cash, guns, and drugs found at the scene.

Rick was lucky to survive the crash relatively unharmed, and in a few days, he was discharged from the hospital. His lawyer then called him at home with some very horrible news. The charges of vehicular assault were now being changed to vehicular homicide. The driver of the car he had hit had lost his life from the crash.

Rick was charged with four felonies, including vehicular homicide. Tried and convicted, he was sentenced on all four counts to twelve years in prison. Rick's father had found Jesus during his time in prison, and it was in prison that Rick also found salvation through Jesus. Sitting in his cell, he had plenty of time to ponder all the choices he had made that brought him to that place in his life. He knew that unless he changed, he would continue on the same trajectory as many of those he grew up with.

Rick felt called out by God, as if He were forcing him to take a hard look at his life and consider his choices. He had to accept the consequences of his previous actions and commit to change before he could move forward on a new path.

When I sat in Bill's office that day, the day I told my Painted Baby Story, I also felt called out. I wasn't sitting in a jail cell weighed down with four felonies and the guilt of taking a man's life weighing on my shoulders. But, like Rick, I wasn't being the man I wanted to be. It wasn't until Bill called me out by challenging me to tell him my worst business story that I was forced to take a hard look at myself too— who I was as a business owner and as a human. After telling my story to Bill, I could never go back to being just a shiny marketing brochure of perfection. I had to own up to my mistakes, consider them, and commit to being a better person. I had to stop hiding behind the Matt I wanted people to see and own up to being the Matt I really was. If I wasn't happy with the real Matt, I couldn't just change the façade—I had to change myself.

Rick, called out by God, considered his life and how it would continue on its current trajectory, and he committed to change, devoting himself to living up to God's standards. Challenged by Bill, I considered my business messaging too, and I committed to stop pretending to be someone I was not. I had to come clean with myself and with others about my bad choices, my mistakes, and everything else that I had been hiding from the world.

How about you? How have these stories called you out? How are you currently presenting yourself as a leader and business owner to your clients, your team, your people? Are there any places in your business where you feel called out? If so, they may be big things, or they may be small. Whatever the size and scope, let's talk about the Three C's of Changing Your Story.

THE THREE C'S OF CHANGING YOUR STORY

At its core, this book is about storytelling. More so, this book is to challenge you as to the story you are telling, living, and promoting, and if you need to change it, not the entire story, but maybe just the bits and pieces of it that are preventing you from connecting on a deeper level with others. If you think back to the stories you've read and heard throughout your life, you'll find common elements. At its most basic, every story has a protagonist that is challenged, called out, and has an obstacle or struggle placed in front of them. From there, they consider how these obstacles and struggles will affect the trajectory of their future and the future of others. At that point, they commit. They commit to something. It may be changing their story and changing it for the better. It may be the opposite. This is embedded into the framework of a story and the elements required to change your story.

After my meeting with Bill, I realized I had to change my story—the story I told myself and others about who I was and who our company was. But coming to that conclusion happened through a process. After reflecting back on this process, I have organized it into what I call the Three C's of Changing Your Story. They are being Called Out, Consideration, and Commitment to change.

In this chapter, we'll discuss these Three C's and how you can use the framework within them to change your story, both in your business, and in other domains of your life. You may have noticed already that I have referred to your business and your life. In this book, we'll talk about both, because they're connected. You can't run your best business if you're not living your best life. And after all, business is just the process of humans serving each other as they participate in life alongside and with each other.

Let's jump into the Three C's of Changing Your Story.

THE FIRST C: CALLED OUT

One of my passions is Brazilian Jiu Jitsu (BJJ). Previous to discovering and learning this martial art in 2007, my activity of choice was lifting weights at the local Gold's Gym. I always drove past a nearby mixed martial arts gym, curious about what was going on inside. One day, to satisfy that curiosity, I decided to check out the place—and walked in right before a jiu jitsu class.

At this point in my life, I was 210 pounds of pure muscle with a personality to match the muscles. I was full of energy, ego, and attitude, always feeling the need to prove myself. In hindsight, I realize this was sheer insecurity, but at the time I believed that was how "real men" behaved.

When I entered the MMA gym, a man named Noah, who appeared to be one of the instructors, invited me to grapple with one of the students. He instructed me to go grapple another young man, or should I say boy, who appeared to be half my age and size. He was a teenager—maybe fourteen or fifteen and one hundred and twenty pounds at the most.

Noah squeezed my bulging bicep and whispered to me, "Take it easy on him." He then smiled and gave me a couple of large pats on my back, encouraging me to step onto the grappling mats. Looking back, I now know that the smile and smirk on his face were all due to the fact that he knew what was about to happen to me next.

I stepped onto the mat to face off with this kid. Of course, I'd go easy on him—he was so tiny and frail, no match for my bulging biceps, massive muscles, and enormous ego. We slapped hands and bumped knuckles, signaling that we were both ready to engage in combat or as we call it in the jiu jitsu world, "rolling." Wanting to end the engagement quickly so as not to embarrass this little guy, I quickly drove forward, expecting to knock him on his back. In an instant, I was on my back, and he was on top of me. He only weighed 120 pounds but felt like 400 on top of me. His body weight seemed to multiply as he slowly squeezed the life out of me. I could quickly feel my energy, ego, and air fleeing my body. Filled with fear and desperation, I flopped and flailed around the mats, and then turned onto my stomach to attempt to shake off this 120-pound piece of human Velcro. As soon as I turned onto my stomach, he placed his arms around my neck and gently squeezed. In this moment, I remembered Noah telling me just minutes before that if I wanted my opponent to stop whatever he was doing to "tap out," which is the action of tapping your hand a couple of times on your opponent signaling you give up. As I recalled that conversation, I quickly felt the blood to my brain being shut off. Faced with only one option, being choked unconscious, I tapped out.

Angry and humiliated, I first let the blood rush back to my brain, then sprang to my feet, swallowed my pride, and tried again. We slapped hands, bumped knuckles, and this time, I went at the kid with even more force.

Again, I was quickly thrown to my back and found myself with this kid, AGAIN, sitting in the mounted position on top of me. But before the teenager could get his scrawny hands on my neck again to choke me, I pushed him away in a strong bench press–like motion. Like a spider monkey, he latched onto one of my arms and spun his body around my arm in a tight circle. He then fell off the side of my body executing an arm lock known as an armbar. Unable to move, and faced with only one option, my arm breaking, I was forced to tap out AGAIN.

Now even more angry, more humiliated, and on the verge of crying, I tried again and again to pin this kid, to dominate this kid, to beat this kid, but every engagement ended the same. We rolled about six or seven times before I finally threw my hands up in the air and gave up for the day completely. Frustrated, I asked, "How are you doing this?"

"I'm just using your own weight, strength, energy, and resources against you. Pretty cool, isn't it?"

I was hooked. On this most embarrassing day, I decided to embark on my journey to learn Brazilian Jiu Jitsu and have been practicing ever since.

This introduction to BJJ challenged everything I believed about size, strength, and power. My weight and muscle strength were no match against someone smaller and weaker who knew how to use proper leverage and technique against me.

I was called out that day. Called out by Noah, called out by this young kid, and called out internally—being challenged to rethink my beliefs, to reconsider an assumption I'd adopted as truth. That truth, as it turned out, was completely false.

Every day in business, we make decisions based on beliefs and assumptions. When those beliefs and assumptions are challenged, we get called out. Being called out, no matter how uncomfortable it makes us feel, shouldn't be avoided, but welcomed. When our beliefs are challenged and called out, we have an opportunity to question them and see whether they hold water. We may be challenged in a way that totally breaks down our belief to disbelief. We also must evaluate whether we hold empowering, solid, and positive beliefs that serve and elevate us. Or do we hold the opposite: disempowering ones that sabotage us and hold us back from living our true and best story.

My belief that clients just wanted to see my shiny marketing brochure was wrong. Rick's belief that his life leading up to prison was on the right path was wrong. And that day on the jiu jitsu mat, my belief that my size, strength, and ego could overpower a skinny teenager was so wrong, it was embarrassing.

What are you being called out on at the moment? What beliefs and assumptions are you holding onto and carrying within your business that have been challenged recently? Who has challenged them or been a catalyst to have you challenge them? Have you recently been thrown down to your back and had the life choked out of you, and can't figure out why? Maybe you didn't land that last big deal you were certain you would land. Maybe a team member you swore would work with you forever just up and quit your company.

Remember that as uncomfortable as being called out is, it is absolutely necessary to grow in business and in life. When you face being called out, the next logical step is the second C, Consideration.

THE SECOND C: CONSIDERATION

Remember Dave Albin? I met Dave, owner of Firewalk Adventures, in 2014. Dave's company performs life-changing experiences for small business owners, entrepreneurs, and corporations around the world. Dave woke up the morning of June 8th, 1988, grossly addicted to alcohol and drugs. He had come to a point in his life where living with the devastating emotional and physical pain associated with these addictions needed to end. So, to end it, Dave went to his bedroom, loaded a pistol, and put it in his mouth.

But then, Dave considered his actions and how they would play out for those around him.

Just as Dave was about to pull the trigger, he began thinking about his kids. They would probably find him. He considered what that would be like for them, and how it would affect them and their lives. Dave considered that maybe he had other options. He decided to find a better place to do it, so he went into the woods. Each time, as he was getting ready to pull the trigger, he'd think about his kids again, and his wife. But the pain was overwhelming, and he had to do something to end it. Dave put the gun in his mouth and took it out, over and over again, considering his options. Trying to decide if he even had other options. Dave now returned to his living room couch, and realized he had a gun in one hand and a telephone in the other. Dave then cast his attention to the telephone. Was this the lifeline he needed? As Dave was considering his options, he decided to put the gun down and called Alcoholics Anonymous.

That moment of consideration was a turning point for Dave. He got clean and sober for himself and his family, and he eventually went on to start Firewalk Adventures where he has impacted the lives of thousands of other people.

Internalization, Visualization, and Destination

Consideration consists of three steps that we will discuss here. These steps are internalization, visualization, and destination. Consideration is taking time and space to rethink and reevaluate your beliefs, your assumptions, your options, and your future desired direction and outcome, which will then lead you to action. Consideration could happen in one second, ten seconds, ten days, or ten years. During that time, you consider the trajectory of your current path. You look at where that path is taking you and whether it's where you really want to go. The deeper or more important the change to consider, the longer it could take one to make.

Consideration is the pivot point where you evaluate your next move. You can pack up your shiny marketing brochure and go home, or you can tell your PBS. You can continue on a self-destructive path that negatively impacts those around you or turn your life around and embrace a better way. You can keep tapping out by trying to take down someone who may not be bigger, but knows exactly how to take you down, or you can step off the mat and admit you have much to learn.

Internalization

When was the last time you were called out? Do you remember how it felt? At the moment of receiving a callout, for me, it felt like a hit to the gut. One in which I needed to take in and deal with for a minute.

The first part of consideration is internalization. This is the step in which you sit with the callout for a minute. You do not act on it or make any decisions about it; you just take it all in. This internalization will allow you to play out the next two steps, which are visualization and destination.

When I was repeatedly choked out by that young child on the jiu jitsu mats, I took a minute after class to take it all in. I walked away, defeated, with my head down, back to my car and just sat there for a few minutes. I took in all the sounds, sights, and emotions of what had just happened. I replayed the scenario out in my mind and how this scenario called me out over and over. In doing so, I went through the range of emotions that came with that. Before I was to act or make any decisions, I just needed it all to sink in. From there, this is where you will head into the next step of visualization.

Visualization

Visualization happens after you have had the time to internalize and take everything in. Visualization involves playing out the current scenario and what it looks like if it continues to move in the same direction into the future.

Play out the current scenario into the future. Paint a picture of what your life and business will look like one, three, five, and even ten years from now if you stay on this same path. Is this the desired outcome you wish for?

Here it is important to realistically play out your current scenario into the potential outcomes (destinations) you will be taken to. Back to my jiu jitsu example, after I took the time to internalize what just happened, I continued to play out what had just transpired into the future. What would my training look like if I continued to come to jiu jitsu class and just drive forward with all my size, speed, and strength? What outcome would that produce for me? Where would my current trajectory, mindset, attitude, and belief system bring me?

Destination

Destination is where you arrive through the visualization process. It is the end outcome of your decision to continue on the same path you are on, the path you were called out about. When you arrive at this destination, will you be happy and pleased with it? Will it be a good thing or a bad thing? Will it elevate and improve your business and life or do the opposite? The last key component to consideration is deciding if the destination to which you are headed is an acceptable one or not. If not, then committing to change must happen.

In your business, you may be called out by someone else, like a team member or a client. Or you may be called out by a number on a report that shows you aren't making enough profit to run a sustaining company. Sometimes you have to call yourself out. Maybe you've just fired the third team member for the same problem—and you haven't stopped to consider that maybe it's not the people you fired, but you, who is the common denominator and root of the issue.

Business people, and especially business owners, spend a lot of time "doing the work": repeating the same activities we've done over and over again, without giving them much thought. We like to be productive, and doing the work produces results and revenue. We get caught up in the "busy-ness of business." We don't always set aside the time and the space for intentional consideration of what's going on in our businesses, including considering the callouts. These callouts are easy to push aside, bury with busy-ness, or just plain ignore. Intentional, evaluation, and consideration are really hard work. It's where we should be spending more of our time, so we can make better decisions that will improve our future outcomes in life and business. Consideration is all about prevention now rather than needing intervention later.

THE THIRD C: COMMIT TO CHANGE

Dave Albin decided to take the gun out of his mouth and out of his hand. He then made a phone call to Alcoholics Anonymous. That phone call was the beginning of his journey toward a new life of sobriety and freedom. After that call, Dave was picked up by a man named Loren who took Dave to his first AA meetings. During his first meetings, he was showered with love and support as he opened up to a group of people who were experiencing many of the same hurts, pains, and addictions he was.

After being called out and spending much time considering his options that fateful June 1988 morning, Dave decided and committed to changing his life and getting clean and sober. Today he is celebrating his 34th year of sobriety. When I spoke to Dave about his journey and how he was able to stay on track he shared this:

This commitment for me required a lot of hard work and I was willing to do the work and was up for the challenge. After that commitment, the work began. I was plugged into a very loving and supportive group of people that challenged and encouraged me along the way. I am so glad I made the commitment I did that day.

The Work Begins After Your Commitment

Committing to change takes effort. You have to make a conscious decision to do it, and then actually follow through with your actions. Too often, even though we see that our current path isn't getting the desired results—and sometimes, that path is actually sabotaging our results—we stubbornly stick to the same old way of doing things. This sounds ridiculous, right? Why would we keep making the same mistakes that put us on a trajectory toward failure?

Change is hard. It takes discipline. It takes action. It takes getting out of the same rut you've been following for months, years, or maybe your entire life. Sometimes the change we need to make requires the breaking of habits or beliefs that have been deeply ingrained in us. We are used to walking the same path day after day, month after month, year after year. After careful consideration, you have a decision to make. Don't make it lightly. Be honest with yourself about that decision and where it will lead you. If staying the same is taking you down a path you know will lead to a destination you do not wish to arrive at, do whatever it takes to commit to change. Declare it out loud. Write it down. Have a conversation with someone you care about and tell them about how you were called out, and your consideration process. Tell them you're going to change. If you can't do this yourself, ask them to hold you accountable.

My commitment to change happened after my meeting with Bill.

I declared my intentions to my team, and though they thought I had lost my mind in the moment, committing to change how I did business out loud like that made it real. It reinforced my commitment. Rick, sitting in his prison cell, declared his commitment to change to God, dedicated his life to God, and then aligned his actions moving forward with this commitment. Dave Albin made his commitment to sobriety first to himself and then to the group of people in his first meeting.

Commitment to change is a decision. Commitment to change is a promise. Commitment to change requires action and continued action. Commitment to change requires continued accountability. Maybe you have been reading this section and know there is something you need to commit to. It may be big; it may be small. Right now, before you move on, I want you to commit. Remember, I've got your back!

· · ·

NOT JUST THE BIG STUFF

The Three C's of Changing Your Story don't just happen with large decisions, such as the ones Rick and Dave made. They come up with small decisions too. They happen at both the macro and micro level. Many times, the micro decisions, and small decisions we continue to make, will cause a macro-sized problem that will need to be addressed in the future. It can be as simple as the small voice in the back of your head asking: *should I keep scrolling through the social media feeds or put my phone down?* Or *do I want to eat this cheeseburger today?* Or, *do I want to keep working for another hour when I know I promised my family I would be home?*

Although seemingly small decisions, you are still working through the process of calling yourself out, considering a new decision, and then making that decision and committing to it. As you're taking that time for intentional consideration of what's going on in your business, including the callouts, don't overlook the micro-level decisions and changes along with the macro-level ones. Small changes can have a dramatic impact on your business.

These Three C's happen in life all the time. Bill made me realize it. Rick and Dave's experiences made them realize it. It changed all three of our lives in impactful ways. Not only that, but we realized that small decisions led up to our large moments of realization. Sometimes the callout isn't loud enough; sometimes you need to be bashed over the head with it. The strength and volume of the callout must be proportional to the thing it's trying to change. If Rick had remained on his path, he may not have survived. It took a dramatic event—a loud and clear callout—to get his attention. However, his downfall wasn't caused by one bad decision, but by a number of micro-decisions that brought him to a place of a large and life-altering decision.

As a business owner, you may not ever face a challenge that could end your life, but you may be called out on issues that could end your business. Imagine discovering that you can't make payroll. Major callout, right? You didn't suddenly run out of money though—you made a number of small decisions over time that led to the lack of funds. If you had listened closely to those smaller callouts, you may have corrected the impending disaster before it was too late.

Now that you have heard my PBS, as well as Rick and Dave's stories, including the calling out, our considerations, and our commitments to change, I have a question for you. What part of your story, in your business and your life, needs to change? Where do you need to be called out? What parts of your business, if continued to operate in the manner in which they are operating, are slowly (or quickly) taking you to an undesired destination? Are you ready to change? If so, let's commit. Let's change that story. Before we get to that point, let's talk about how to explore your story more.

If you are still curious about or questioning the importance of stories and their significance, let's roll on to Chapter 3.

PAINTED BABY WORKBOOK FUN RESOURCE

Be sure to download the free Painted Baby workbook. I created a video reenactment of exactly how I was beat up repeatedly by that young kid on the jiu jitsu mats. It is located in the Chapter 2 fun resource section of the book.

→ https://www.mattshoup.com/free-tools/

QUESTIONS TO CONSIDER

1. How have you been called out lately? Who has challenged you in life and in business? Which beliefs or assumptions have been challenged?

2. Have you considered how your business and life will play out in the future on this path? What if you changed? How will that play out?

3. In her book *The 5 Second Rule*, Mel Robbins claims that when faced with a major decision, the choice you make in the first five seconds matters. She argues that the longer you take to consider and overanalyze, the more you'll try to protect yourself from harm and will ultimately fall back into old patterns.[1] Do your major decisions tend to change after the first five seconds? Why? What if you gave that initial choice a try? How might that impact your life, your business, and your direction?

4. Think about all the recent callouts you've experienced. Start writing them down as they happen. Then spend some time thinking—giving these callouts the consideration they—and you—deserve.

5. How can you implement time and space in your business and life to execute the Three C's of Changing Your Story? How can you be proactive about this process?

1 Mel Robbins, *The 5 Second Rule: Transform your Life, Work, and Confidence with Everyday Courage* (New York: Savio Republic, 2017).

CHAPTER 3

EXPLORING YOUR STORY

One of my favorite childhood memories was tuning in to Saturday morning professional wrestling. I admired World Wrestling Federation (WWF), now World Wrestling Entertainment (WWE), heroes of the 1980s like Hulk Hogan and the Ultimate Warrior as they battled it out in the ring. I admittedly was a fan of professional wrestling all the way through high school. Transitioning from the 1980s to the '90s, I remember following stars such as Stone Cold Steve Austin and The Rock.

About five years ago, I was watching some videos on YouTube when a video popped up with the title "The Simple Message that Brought this Middle School Class to Tears." I noticed the video had millions of views, as well as remembered this video had popped up across my other social media platforms in the past. So, I decided to click on it and give it a watch.

The speaker was Marc Mero. I immediately remembered him from the days of the WWE in the '90s. Marc had moved on from professional wrestling and was now a motivational speaker who addressed middle school and high school kids on the topic of anti-bullying. Marc talked about his relationship with his mom and how, in his high school days, she went to every one of his football games, where she ran up and down the sidelines cheering on her son.

Marc went on to share that as his mother loved and supported him, he decided to run with the wrong crowd, frequently getting drunk and high. He shared how he almost overdosed on drugs three times and how his life as a professional wrestler was all about chasing fame and money. All the while, as Marc was chasing glamour, fame, and fortune, he grew apart from his family and forgot about how much his mother had supported him early on. He lost sight of how important that relationship had been to him.

Marc's career as a professional wrestler took him around the world. One day, on the road in Japan, he got a phone call. His mother had passed away. Marc was on the other side of the world and hadn't seen anyone in his family in a long time. He was focused on himself and his career, but losing his mother brought what was truly important into sharp focus for him. By then, it was too late to make up for all the time he had lost. Important relationships had been ignored and he had instead squandered his life on things that didn't matter. Marc made a commitment to change. Marc's story brought his young audience to tears, and I have to admit, I began to tear up just watching the video.[2]

Marc explored his story and decided to change his story using the lessons he learned from it to make an impact in the lives of young people. If you need to change your story, and you choose not to, you may be wasting an opportunity to make a bigger impact with those

2   Marc Mero, "The Simple Message That Brought This Middle School Class to Tears," *The Powerful Message About A Mother's Love*, YouTube video, 4:38, December 29, 2014, https://www.youtube.com/watch?v=WI0Twlt1aek

your business serves. But you must be willing, like Marc, to peel back the layers and explore your story at a deeper level.

THE IMPORTANCE OF EXPLORING YOUR STORY

When I started this book, I initially titled this chapter, "Your Story Matters." However, I realized as I was writing it that when you focus only on the importance of your *own* story, you might underestimate the importance of the stories of others. It's not always about you, or about me. This is an important concept to consider in any human interaction, and it plays a significant part in leadership. Leaders who fail to consider the stories of others with whom they interact miss out on opportunities to learn and to grow, and their ability to connect is greatly diminished.

A TOOL TO HELP EXPLORE YOUR STORY: THE JOHARI WINDOW

The Johari window is a psychological tool created by Joseph Luft and Harry Ingham in 1955. The model is used to help individuals better understand themselves and how they are perceived by others. This tool is used in exercises to help others deepen their relationships and gain more self-awareness. It is used in many professional settings as a team development tool. It is known to deepen interpersonal communication and relationships between teams and groups. The cool thing about this model is that it inspires us to be more authentic, genuine, and open with each other, allowing us to form deeper connections. This is a window into your behavior, personality, and belief systems. I was first introduced to this technique and tool as part of an Entrepreneur's Organization Forum retreat that I attended.

The Johari window comprises four segments or panes, which describe the following:

1. What you know and others know (open area or arena). Also known as: *I know and you know.*

2. What you know that others don't know (façade or hidden window). Also known as: *I know but you don't know.*

3. What you don't know but others know (blind spot). Also known as: *I don't know but you do know.*

4. What no one knows (unknown). Also known as: *Nobody knows.*

Not only does this tool help us to better understand ourselves and others, but it also can be used as a framework to determine which parts of our stories we share with others. What we share in our stories falls into one of these four categories. For example, I could share that my name is Matt and I'm a business owner and an author. I am open and outgoing, full of energy, and love to drink Spanish coffee. I know this, you know this, and it falls into the first category of what we both know, the open window. I'm 100 percent comfortable sharing this information in a story. There is no risk by sharing it as everybody knows it.

Here's a tidbit from the second category (the façade): I like to drink whiskey, and a few years ago, I was drinking *way* too much of it. You didn't know that about me but now you do. Sharing that information was riskier than telling you my name is Matt. It was information that only I knew, and you didn't until I shared it with you. Now, that information has been transferred to the open window. There was a time, place, and space in which I was ready to share that information with you. My Painted Baby Story fit into this category until I decided to share it.

In the third category, blind spot, maybe you see something that I do not. I might add that I was drinking too much whiskey to be sociable with others—all those business acquaintances. You might call me out right there, pointing out that I was working too much at that time and I was using whiskey as a crutch to escape the pressure, instead of dealing with it in a more productive and healthier manner.

If you were correct in that statement and I realized it, this information would also move into the known window or pane. I would also learn from that, grow from it, and if you delivered that information in a non-judgmental, caring way because you have my best interest at heart, our bond might strengthen.

The fourth category, the unknown, is just that. It is information that none of us know. At first glance, this may just seem like a never-changing window, that we should be okay with this unknown. The really fun and intriguing part of the Johari window is that the more of your façade you share with others, making it known, combined with the more you discover about yourself that was not known with the help of others (blind spot), the smaller the unknown window becomes. The more you can move information into the known, the more you can be aware of and ready to share your story with others.

We all want to paint the best possible versions of ourselves but doing so is about as productive as designing a shiny marketing brochure. There is no learning, no growth, and no connection. To create that trust, we must be willing to tear away the pretty pages and replace them with a few tattered ones, even if we don't understand what those tattered pages mean or where they exist.

PEELING BACK THE LAYERS OF YOUR STORY

Stories have deep roots and many layers. Personal histories are passed down to us. Your own history and lived experiences are brought from the past into the now, both in business and life. These all impact and build your story. You take the things that have been imprinted upon you and impart them to others as you experience life and business with them.

When you start to peel back and understand your own story from a different perspective, you can achieve clarity about where you are *now*. You can learn how you currently operate in life and business, as well as where some of your behaviors, actions, and beliefs come from, and how they affect other people.

That's the power and importance of exploring your story.

TERRI COOMER

Meet Terri Coomer. Terri is the former owner and CEO of Live, Love & Laugh Homecare. She and her wife, Patty, launched their company from $8,000 and a dream and grew it into a large and successful senior care company. Driven by a passion for helping people live life to the fullest, love unconditionally, and laugh with abandon, they started their business in 2009 with just one caregiver on staff. When they sold it in 2022, they had twenty-six caregivers, three full-time office staff, and a full-time CEO and COO.

When I sat down with Terri to hear her story, she had sold the business and she and her wife were retired. At the time, I was reaching out to business owners to have them share their Painted Baby Stories. Terri came into my office, and we sat down to enjoy some Spanish coffee and catch up. I met Terri almost twenty years earlier when she was working alongside my wife at an elderly respite care facility. I thought I knew her whole story, but it wasn't until this conversation that she peeled back the layers for me.

Initially, my goal was to hear Terri's PBS, and she did tell it, and I will share it with you later in this book. But I learned much more in that conversation. Terri told me about what really motivated her to succeed in business. Earlier in her life, she had been active in sports. She also had a very critical stepfather. She would get four hits out of five times at bat in a softball game, and instead of celebrating the four hits, her stepdad would come down on her for the one time she didn't hit the ball and make it to first base. As Terri told the story, she recalled how painful those experiences had been. She took his critical comments to heart and believes they are what drove her to find something in which she could succeed with no room for criticism. Decades after Terri left home, after she had built and sold a very successful business, her stepfather finally told her that he was proud of her. Terri became very emotional at this point in our conversation and confessed that she had gone to therapy years earlier to deal with her stepfather's criticism.

Terri's story wasn't a business story; it was a life story. But her willingness to be vulnerable connected us in a way we had never connected before. I felt honored that she trusted me enough to share, and of course, I asked her permission to share her story in this book.

The more you can get perspective on your own story and where you sit within it, the better you'll be able to relate with others in your business. This involves peeling back the layers of unknowns and exposing your blind spots. In order to expose these blind spots, many times, you will continue to view your story possibly through different perspectives while asking yourself "What is missing? What have I not yet learned and observed? Do I see something now that I have not seen before?" Sometimes, this process involves having another person walk through your story with you while asking questions that you may have never considered. This additional perspective will assist you in peeling back layers of your story you may have never known existed, which in turn exposes more of your story to you.

You have to be vulnerable, and you have to trust the process. To what degree have you peeled back the layers and dug into the roots of your story? How is it playing out in your business, your leadership, and your interactions with your team? Could you do better if you looked deeper? By exploring your story from the past up to the present, you may be surprised by what you discover that can add more value to your story of the future.

BATTLING PERFECTION

Everybody puts their best faces, lives, families, vacations, and highlights out there for the world to see. If you don't believe me, just scroll through one of your social media feeds.

This behavior should come as no surprise. From an early age, we're conditioned to be perfect, or to achieve as close a state of perfection as possible. TV commercials pitch products that make us look better, live better, feel better, even smell better. The personal development industry is booming. Whether it's weight loss or Botox, there's a quick and easy way for you to make yourself "better," just waiting for...your hard-earned dollars. While some of these products may actually bring positive results, the problem with all of them is that you will never be perfect. And someone, somewhere, will always be out there reminding you that you're still not...quite...good enough. You can always do better, live better, be...*better*. But think about it. What is perfection? Who is perfect? Has anyone ever really achieved that state? Never mind perfection; if we all even attained a state of contentment and being "good enough," these industries that capitalize on our insecurities would go broke. They can't afford to let us think for even one minute that we're okay just as we are.

If you are of this mindset—always thinking you're not good enough—don't feel bad about it. We're all in the same boat, because we've been trained to think that way our whole lives. But we can undo that training. We can embrace those "negative" qualities in ourselves, which aren't really negatives at all, but part of our uniqueness, our very *humanness*, and share them with the world. These are our truths, and they have power.

WHY WE SHARE OUR STORIES

Harvard University conducted a study where they analyzed how our brains react to speaking about ourselves versus speaking about others. They hooked up participants to an MRI and compared their brain activity under these different circumstances. When the talk included self-disclosure, higher levels of activation in the medial prefrontal cortex occurred, a part of the brain that's associated with self-related thoughts. This activation made sense.

However, two other regions of the brain also lit up: the nucleus accumbens (NACC) and the ventral tegmental area (VTA). Both of these areas are part of the mesolimbic dopamine system: our feel-good rewards. Those systems are also linked to pleasurable feelings and states associated with stimuli such as sex, cocaine, and good food.

The fact that the NACC and VTA lit up during self-disclosure suggests that talking about ourselves is inherently pleasurable. People are naturally motivated to tell their stories and self-disclose. So, what stops us from sharing our true stories?

THE CLOUD OF FEAR, SHAME, GUILT, AND JUDGMENT

One of my favorite TED Talks of all time is from Brené Brown. Brené refers to herself as a researcher and storyteller who has spent a large portion of her professional career researching vulnerability. In doing so, she has been able to gather results and data around something that all of us as humans experience, journey through, and struggle with, and oftentimes, have a hard time quantifying. One of the reasons we do not show up as our authentic selves is because we are overridden with the fear of shame, guilt, and being judged by others.

In Brené's TED Talk, she explains that we as humans are neurobiologically wired for connection as it gives purpose and meaning to our lives. She also explains that shame unravels connection. Shame is the voice inside of you that says, "Is there something about me that, if others know or see, will show that I am not worthy of connection?" But the truth is for connection to happen, we have to allow ourselves to be seen. Brené states that excruciating vulnerability is what can conquer shame. She explains that vulnerability occurs when people let go of who they thought they should be to embrace who they truly are.

So, why don't we do it? Fear is the likely culprit. All that perfection training has gotten to us to the point that we're afraid that if we project anything other than an ideal and perfect, put together person, we'll suffer some kind of repercussions. We'll be embarrassed, humiliated, rejected, abandoned, spurned. Choose a verb—there are so many of them and we don't know how other people will react, so the unpredictability makes us even more reluctant to open up and show the world who we really are inside.

Whatever you're hiding can be used to your advantage, but only if you allow it to be looked at from a different angle. Seek to better understand it. Try to think about it with more information and context. Be brave enough to share it and ask for others' perspectives. All those warts you're hiding can serve—instead of sabotage—you. Instead of holding you back, they can move you forward, but you must first understand and accept them. Once you understand and accept your true story, telling it becomes much easier. An added benefit is that others will observe you doing this and be inspired and encouraged to do the same.

People in leadership positions may be reluctant to share information about themselves that could cast them in a negative light. After all, there's a lot on the line, and they require the respect of others to fulfill their positions as business owners, teachers, managers, role models, and so forth. This results in creating an impenetrable space between themselves and everyone else, but that space must be breached in order to build trust. When a leader finds the courage to let people know that they are not perfect, that they have stories in their lives that illustrate just how imperfect—how human—they truly are, they don't lose the respect of others. Rather, they are inviting people into that space where they can then relax, put down their guard, and allow themselves to be human too. This is how and where trust begins and connections form.

Remember as you take a brave step into this space: Be vulnerable. Be human. Be you. Create that space with another person and *connect*.

STORIES AND LEADERSHIP

I wrote this book for you, as well as all the other people you serve in business. Your story matters, their story matters, and the more you can connect to the stories of those you are responsible for leading and serving, the better your life and business will become. Just as in the case with Marc, you have the opportunity to connect with these individuals in your life and business at a deeper and more meaningful level. You have an opportunity to learn more about yourself by sharing your story, and to help others learn about themselves by listening to their stories.

Stories allow us to connect on a deeper level than is possible with the typical discussions we all share in our day-to-day lives, where we talk about the weather, the latest movie we saw, or the last book we read. We give up a piece of "us" and in return, we get a little bit of someone else. We get their perspective on us, and vice versa. But only if we choose to interact. We must listen, think, and respond. Not by moving on to the next subject, or competing for attention with a better story, but by intentionally listening, accepting without judgment, and offering our thoughts. Connecting with other people is perhaps the most human thing we do in life. Stories make it possible.

PAINTED BABY WORKBOOK RESOURCES

If you haven't already, download the free Painted Baby workbook. In it, I have included the links to both Marc Mero and Brené Brown's videos. They are located in the Chapter 3 resources section.

→ https://www.mattshoup.com/free-tools/

QUESTIONS TO CONSIDER

1. Which parts of your story are known to you and known to others (open)?

2. Which parts of your story are known to you but not to others (façade)?

3. What is your current comfort level of sharing one of those façade items with somebody?

4. What part of your story might be known to others but not to you (blind spots)?

5. What is your greatest fear in sharing untold parts of your stories with others?

6. What do you think would happen and how do you think others would respond if you began sharing some of these parts of your story?

CHAPTER 4

TESTING MY HYPOTHESIS

Back in Chapter 1, I told you my Painted Baby Story, and how sharing it with Bill changed how I interacted with people and how I did business.

I didn't give you the whole story, and what transpired after this encounter with Bill.

Walking into Bill's office that day, I was a hyper-sales-focused, close-the-deal kind of guy. I believed the key to being a successful business owner was always having the right answer and the right sales pitch. But what happened that day short-circuited my belief system around sales, business, and relationships.

Recall that I went back to the office and discussed the deal with my team. They wanted to know every detail, and together, we dissected the whole meeting and unanimously concluded that the only difference between that sales encounter and the hundreds of other sales calls we had done was the PBS.

I developed a hypothesis that letting down my guard, casting away the "salesguy Matt" persona, and getting real as a person with Bill had allowed him to see me for who I really was, and still am: someone who stands behind their word and is willing to share their shortcomings and failures. A guy who makes mistakes but takes responsibility for them. A business owner dedicated to getting the project done right, no matter how many obstacles get in the way. I knew then that I should share more of my vulnerable, not-so-perfect moments. I had to share this Painted Baby Story more.

Could what happened with Bill be repeated with other clients? I had to know. I told my team my plans and they were skeptical. Was I really going to do this? They'd seen me try crazy marketing tactics. Some worked—one in particular, the rockstar roadside sign spinner, for example—and others did not, like the M & E Painting urinal cakes at a popular bar and restaurant. When we started getting calls in the middle of the night from people who were obviously inebriated, we decided that urinal cakes weren't the best way to reach our target audience. But hey, I will try anything once.

The PBS wasn't a marketing tactic though. And it wasn't just another clever close. Telling my Painted Baby Story was different because it created the opportunity to change the relationship and conversation between myself and a potential client. It opened the door to build deeper trust.

Building trust between people, especially between people who represent business and the clients they serve, is a slow process. I wondered if I could accelerate the process by changing how I spoke with and related to my clients. What if I stopped showing them only my shiny marketing brochure, and told them about the times when a project didn't work out as planned? What if I told them that my business had made some mistakes? What if I told them my best worst story—my PBS?

I had to test my theory. Whether it worked or not, I had to know, and the only way to know for sure was to repeat the story with more prospective clients.

TAKING MY STORY ON THE ROAD

The week that I logged that $60,000 project on the whiteboard, I still had eight more sales calls to go on my calendar. I saw these as eight opportunities to test out my hypothesis. My close rate at the time was 45 percent.

On my next upcoming appointment, I was called to provide a home painting proposal for a nice young couple. I started off the same way I always had: made a confirmation call to make sure the client knew I was coming, showed up on time, went through a discovery process to figure out what they needed, and recited M & E Painting's benefit checklist. At this point, I would usually break out the shiny marketing brochure. Instead, I did something different.

"Here's the proposal," I explained. "But before we get into those details, I just want to share something with you that most companies will not share. I want to be upfront with you about how not every project goes as planned, even for my company." Then I recounted the Painted Baby Story.

The couple listened intently, fully engaged in the story, just as Bill had been. But this time, when I pushed the contract and a pen across the table and asked for the business, they didn't agree to do business. We continued with the conversation, and I attempted to discover what objections they might have. They said the famous words, "We would like to think about it," and they would get back to me.

No big deal, I thought, thanking them for their time, shaking their hands, and saying I'd look forward to hearing from them. This was a typical response from some of the people I gave proposals to, and I figured I would follow up in a few days. After all, I had seven more calls to go that week, and I only needed three or four to maintain my average close rate.

It wasn't to be. My second call went the same way as the first, and so did the third. I was determined, though—the story had worked so well with Bill. It had to work again. Yet, the fourth, fifth, sixth, seventh, and eighth calls all ended the same. Eight calls, no sales.

REFINING MY THEORY

At the next company meeting with my team, I got a good bit of teasing.

"How'd that Painted Baby Story go?" they asked. They told me that what happened with Bill was a fluke and I shouldn't try it again. It was ruining my sales. I was ruining my *business*.

I thought about how I was telling my story to these new clients compared to how I had shared it with Bill. And realized that before telling Bill about my painting mishaps, I had, actually, shown him my marketing brochure. With the eight trials that followed, I had been so eager to share my PBS that I had skipped the shiny marketing brochure, all the good stuff, completely. Those clients never got a chance to see all the great work my company had done, or the wonderful feedback from my satisfied clients.

That shiny marketing brochure reflected my team's capabilities and my business's success. It showcased our best work and gave proof, with client reviews. Bill had taken issue with me showing him ONLY the brochure and expecting him to trust me based on that one-sided image of perfection. I was asking these people to trust me based on an equally lopsided image of my worst day in business.

Telling my Painted Baby Story wasn't enough. I had to balance it with my best *best* stories too, and I had to tell it at the right time and in the right way. I worked on capturing the important details, crafting them in a way that made sense to my potential clients, and communicating them more clearly. Later in the book, Part Two, I will introduce you to another Three Cs. These are the Three C's of Storytelling. Combined with the Three C's of Changing Your Story, they make up the Six C's of Brave and Vulnerable Storytelling.

I refined my sales approach, starting with the one I had been using for years, but with a slight change. After the discovery, and after showing my brochure, I would say something like this:

"I've presented everything you're looking for. I shared the features and the benefits. You can see we're an established, reputable company." At this point, I would pause. Clients know when you're going to ask for their business, and this is when that would typically happen. But instead of transitioning to the close, I would offer them a glimpse of another side of my business and myself. The side that wasn't represented in 8 × 10 glossy photographs with catchy taglines. That went something like this:

> "Before I ask you for your business, I just want to share something with you to take away potential fear and concerns. Most other companies will not share this and be so upfront and honest with you, however, I would like to. Here's the deal: as much as we're a successful company, we're not perfect. Sometimes things go sideways, or upside-down. There was actually one time when we accidentally painted a baby. Would you like to hear about that?"

Their reactions were always the same. Their eyes got big, a look of confusion and slight shock, many times accompanied by a smile, and then after a moment, they always said yes. Of course, they wanted to hear about something like this going wrong. People always want to hear about things going wrong. They just don't expect to hear those kinds of stories from the painting contractor who's sitting at their kitchen table trying to win their business.

I would share the story, and then I'd explain that even though this was a terrible mistake that would more than likely never happen again, we had a safety meeting to discuss what happened, how it happened, and what we would do to prevent it from happening again. I would then assure the client that if something didn't meet their expectations, I would take care of it. Just like I had taken care of Mrs. Angelo.

A few weeks after my meeting with Bill, I had ten appointments on my calendar. Six of them closed. A few weeks later, seven. A few weeks later, seven again, and again. I was watching my close rate rise, and rise significantly, over these weeks as I shared my PBS.

SEEING RESULTS

Naturally, my team wanted to know what had changed. They had seen my disastrous week where I lost every sale—what was different? Had I abandoned the PBS and come up with a new way to win business?

No, I told them, I just figured out what to tell clients, and when to tell it, and how to tell it. I was still telling my story while continuing to craft it. I didn't figure this out right away. It took dozens of appointments over several weeks to fine tune my conversations and get my story right—the right details at the right time, and within the right context. My hypothesis—that being vulnerable and trusting prospective clients with my worst story would actually encourage them to trust me—turned out to be true. I was pleased to find out I was right in this assumption, but at the same time, I was surprised too. What I learned went against everything I'd been taught about business, about sales, heck—even about life. I thought I was supposed to be showing everyone my best at all times. That was how you got ahead. That was how you got people to like and accept you. That was what you did to survive. My entire perception of how to put myself out there was flipped upside down.

In the weeks and months that followed, I tracked my close rates. Those five, then six, then seven out of ten to twelve deals that closed weren't a fluke—my close rate stayed steady, about 10 to 15 percent higher than it had been before sharing my Painted Baby Story. More importantly, I had better relationships with my clients. If they didn't like something, they would let me know. They understood that mistakes could happen, but that when they did, I would make them right. I had been open and honest with them, and now they were equally open with me.

I trained my team on the process and they saw similar results. Both our close rate and our referral rate went up. Communication between my team and my clients, and even among the members of my team, improved. That vulnerability, and the trust that followed, was contagious.

Shortly after going through the process of testing my hypothesis and presenting the statistics to my team, I trained everyone so they could repeat the process. A few weeks later, during a company meeting, I saw firsthand the results of that training, displayed by one of my team members. "Travis," though good-natured and upbeat, was also generally quiet and reserved. He had been with the company for almost three years but tended to keep to himself and rarely shared information about his personal life. Still, I would ask him basic questions like "How's everything going? The family doing okay? Did you have a good weekend?" His answer was always the same: "Good."

This particular Monday, Travis came to our meeting looking unusually sad. As usual, I asked him how he was doing and how his weekend had been. Instead of the usual "good," he responded quite differently. For the first time ever, he opened up and shared a little bit about what was going on with his family.

One of his close relatives had cancer, he told us. The two were very close, and he was deeply affected by her condition. Listening to him tell his story was like hearing a foreign language. None of us had ever heard him talk about his life. When he had told us all he was willing to say, I told him how much I appreciated him being willing to share his personal story with us, and that we have always been there for him, but in the past, he had never seemed to want to let us in, and we were just respecting his privacy.

Travis said, "Well, Matt, in the past I never felt comfortable telling you these things. But with this Painted Baby Story, and you encouraging us to be more open and honest about what's really going on in the business and at home, I feel like I can trust people more. I want to talk to people and build those deeper relationships like you talked about. So, from now on, I'm going to try harder to do that." Moving forward, not only did our relationship improve, but so did Travis's closing rate in the business.

THE PAINTED BABY STORYTELLING PROCESS

When and how you share your PBS matters. I discovered that opening up with it too soon killed my chances of connecting with my clients in a meaningful way and earning their trust and business. Not sharing it at all left me right where I was before my encounter with Bill. I want to ensure you have a structure and process to overlay whatever your sales model and relationship building model looks like in your business. Businesses all have their own unique process of capturing a client; however, the majority of these companies' processes contain the following components below. As you review them, consider how they will overlay your sales model for your company.

INTRODUCTION AND RAPPORT BUILDING

In the beginning of any business relationship, there's always an introductory process where you shake hands, say hello, and get to know each other. This is not the time to share your Painted Baby Story. This step is critical, because you have to earn permission to speak, and that requires more conversation to reach a level of rapport and trust. The goal here is to get to know the other person more and evaluate if a business relationship moving forward makes sense for both of you. This process involves asking a lot of questions and searching to see how you can serve your potential client.

If you have not established initial rapport and trust in this step, and then you go on to share your PBS, you will do yourself a disservice. You cannot be vulnerable with someone who doesn't know you, like you, and have a certain amount of trust in you. This step is a mutual, back and forth conversation that will eventually lead to a deeper level of engagement and relationship moving forward.

DISCOVERY PROCESS

Once you have spent some time with initial rapport building, it is time to dig in more specifically as to if and how you can serve your potential client. At this point, you enter into a conversation of discovery.

In order to know if you can serve them in some capacity, and if you're the right fit for their needs, the right questions need to be asked. The discovery process involves asking a lot of questions, but questions more directed to their specific needs and what would constitute a successful engagement for your company to serve their needs.

During this process, you will continue to build rapport and get to know each other. Just be sure you are asking targeted questions to ensure you can serve this person well, and that they are your ideal client.

PRESENT YOUR SOLUTION

This is the step where you will show your potential client why your company is the best to meet their needs. In this step, you will present exactly how you will solve your potential client's issue, what you will deliver, how you will deliver it, and what it will cost.

At this point, this is where you will share your shiny marketing brochure. Here, it is important to share all of your wins, amazing work, and happy customers as well as all of the things that make your company unique and the right company to hire.

Here is where you will paint the picture of almost perfection. Remember, your shiny marketing brochure and story up to this point should all be centered around the needs of your client and how you will serve them. But you don't want to leave them expecting perfection. Doing this is a disservice to you and them. It is the ultimate example of overpromising and then setting yourself up to underdeliver.

Transitioning to the next step is important. Before you ask for their business, it is important to signal your transition with something like:

Before I ask for your business, can I share one more important thing with you? Most companies will not be this up front and honest with you, but I would like to. Would you like to hear about a time when our company:

- Painted a baby?

- Painted the wrong home?

- *Fill in your Painted Baby Story hook here* (we will discuss a great hook later in Part Two).

SHARE YOUR PAINTED BABY STORY

You have now set yourself up in an ideal position to share your PBS. As we move soon into Part Two of the book, I will share with you how to capture, craft, and communicate your PBS. Just remember that this is where and when you will share it in the sales process. Don't worry so much right here and now that you have the most well-polished and practiced story. We will dig into that more in the coming chapters. One big point to consider here is that once you share your PBS, you must tie it back to how you will ultimately serve your customer, imperfections and all. From here you will transition to your close.

After you read through Part Two and start to create and tell your PBS, I would encourage you to come back to this section and review the Painted Baby Storytelling Process.

ASK FOR THEIR BUSINESS

You have now shown your potential client that you are the best person and company to serve them, and that you have been forthcoming with your mistakes. Your willingness to be vulnerable has allowed you to have a deeper conversation and forge a deeper connection. You've shown your client an example of a worst-case scenario and showed them that no matter what, you are a responsible person who stands by your business and takes care of your clients.

Many entrepreneurs miss an opportunity to land business because they simply don't ask for it. Make sure you do not commit this mistake here. As you may know, there are so many ways to ask for the business, so many creative ways to close. Over the years, I have experimented with them all. For me, I prefer a very direct and straightforward ask. However you ask, just ask, and make sure the way you ask works for you.

Just remember, ask for the sale!

QUESTIONS TO CONSIDER

1. Do you currently know your sales statistics for your business? How many sales appointments do you go on per day, per week, per month? How many sales do you capture? It is important to calculate this close ratio before you begin your Painted Baby Storytelling Process.

2. Map out your sales process and how and where you can interject your PBS into it. Not sure exactly what your story is yet? Don't worry; just map the process for now.

3. Be sure once you finish this book and begin to tell your PBS, that you continue to track your close ratios and observe the improvements.

CHAPTER 5

PAINTING THE TOWN

Shortly after testing my hypothesis and stepping away from it with solid winning results, I was sitting at a local coffee shop with one of my marketing vendors. We typically met two to three times per year to discuss my marketing strategy and how effective it was, and then came up with new ideas to put into their direct mail piece. As we sipped our coffees, I shared with him that I wanted to change up the design of our ad, as well as change up the messaging.

"I want to start a Painted Baby campaign. I want to put a picture of a painted baby on the mail piece and direct them to our website where we share the story about the time we painted a baby. I want to share this story at a very large scale," I said.

I thought he was going to have a heart attack, or at least choke on his coffee. I visibly saw the fear, shock, and immediate disagreement in his eyes as my idea passed through his mind.

His reaction was not what I expected. My idea was not well received. Not only was he not in agreement with the idea, but he actually looked visibly upset. He looked at me as if I had lost my mind.

"Matt, what are you talking about? Don't you understand this breaks all the rules of traditional marketing and messaging? This would be business suicide. This is absolutely crazy. I can't let you do this. Better yet, let me save you the trouble now. I am not doing this," he said.

When it comes to getting the word out about my businesses, I've been known to try some pretty crazy ideas. When I find out that something works, I'm a "go big or go home" kind of guy. Sharing my PBS one-on-one with clients was changing my painting business, and I couldn't help but wonder what would happen if I took my story to a bigger audience.

What if I incorporated my PBS into my marketing campaigns? I could put it on all our print ads and mailers. I could even put the Painted Baby on bus stops and benches. This wouldn't be anything like the typical advertising that you see for painting contractors. It would be different, it would absolutely capture people's attention, and it would share more of the real M & E Painting, imperfections and all. And we were ready to share that imperfection not just with client interactions, but with potential new clients and our community as a whole. Deep down, this was just something that I knew would work and that we had to give it a try.

My direct mail vendor over coffee continued to question my sanity and again stated, "This is business suicide, and would be the stupidest thing you've ever done." He refused to accept the order. I shouldn't have been surprised by the reaction. After all, this is not how marketing is supposed to work. I was supposed to be showing glossy photos of perfect paint projects and five-star reviews from happy clients gushing over my work. I had those photos and reviews. Why on earth would I resort to sharing anything otherwise?

The more they pushed back, the more I persisted. I had the data to prove that it worked with my clients, and I believed it would work on a bigger scale, but I needed their help. Yes, I knew that this wasn't what normal and standard advertising was supposed to look like, but I was done being normal and standard. Those other advertisers were showing the same old stuff that companies had been showing for generations, and it all began to look and feel the same. There was nothing different about it, so how could somebody distinguish one company and their message from another?

As much as this vendor and many others objected to my request, I continued pushing and began the process of building our Painted Baby campaign. I did understand their reluctance. They had been doing marketing a certain way for a long time. They knew that I had worked hard to make a name for M & E Painting and were probably concerned for me and for my business. So, I wasn't upset, but I was determined. I wanted the business to be known for something more than just great work. I wanted people to know that we stood for something on a deeper and different level. I knew this would be a way to connect with our clients in a more meaningful way. I also knew that this would be one of the most different and off-the-wall marketing campaigns we had ever attempted.

A NEW MARKETING STRATEGY

In any marketing framework, you have to capture people's attention to start a conversation. In Mike Michalowicz's book *Get Different*,[3] he explains and shares the DAD framework of marketing. The first D is to Differentiate yourself, your approach, and your message to your consumers. Mike states that being the best is not better, and that being different is better. He then shares that you must Attract your

---

3   Mike Michalowicz, *Get Different: Marketing That Can't Be Ignored!* (New York: Penguin, 2021).

ideal potential client (the A) and then Direct (the second D) them to take action.

This Painted Baby Story marketing campaign for sure hit on the first D of being different. We ensured that we would be attracting (A) our ideal client as we would launch this campaign through the same mediums that we were currently using to attract them. We also ensured our call to action would be clear, and easy to track to establish ratios.

I now faced an issue. I needed a way to present the story that would work for print ads and other marketing media. I needed some high-quality imagery that would stand out, grab people's attention, and keep that attention.

I needed a painted baby.

Where the heck could I find a painted baby? My first thought was to Google the term. I found some so-so stock photos but none that really grabbed my attention. I mean, I couldn't actually paint a baby for the campaign...or could I?

Wait a minute, I thought. *I know one of the cutest, most adorable babies of all time. My daughter, Hailey. I wonder if we could paint her?* Hailey was three years old at the time and she happily agreed to help out (as much as a three-year-old could agree). Begin operation paint baby!

I engaged with a local photographer to set up a photo shoot at our office. We purchased a dozen bottles of different colored nontoxic paints, dressed Hailey up in all white clothes, and set up a white backdrop in the garage portion of our office. We then set her up in front of the backdrop and spattered the paint all over her. At first, she enjoyed it. She laughed, she smiled, and she was having a great time. She even picked up some of the paint bottles and painted us a little.

At the end of the shoot, we had taken some of the most priceless and memorable images I have ever seen. We had reproduced our painted baby. By the way, Hailey is the painted baby on the cover of this book. Oh, and another note, when she found out I was writing *Painted Baby* and that she would be on the cover, she asked me for a small royalty for every book that sold for being on the cover. So again, thank you for purchasing this book. From me, and from Hailey. To see all of the photos from the photo shoot visit:

https://www.mattshoup.com/painted-baby-photo-shoot/.

Disclaimer: *No babies were harmed in the making of this marketing campaign.*

I worked with our marketing team to create a landing page where I shared our Painted Baby Story, and from there a call to action to request an estimate was present. This was the biggest campaign for M & E Painting ever, and as much as I believed in it, there was still a degree of unknown regarding how it would be received by the Northern Colorado public. I took one final deep breath, and we launched!

The Painted Baby marketing campaign was not the disaster the professionals told me it would be. Despite all the warnings, it was a success. It got the phone to ring—and ring a lot. It was a conversation starter. People wanted to know what it was about, and it gave my team a foot in the door with new clients.

The PBS helped us connect with more people and because of those connections, we made more sales. After we incorporated it into our advertising, we received inquiries that we could trace directly back to the story and campaign.

A couple's call that came in as a general inquiry led to an appointment. When I arrived at their home, they said that they'd seen the Painted Baby advertisements around town and were intrigued. They wanted to know the story behind the images. I told them the Painted Baby Story and how I had first told it to Bill. Surprisingly, they knew Bill, which added another connecting point to the conversation. Not only that, but after I told them the story, they recalled that Bill had mentioned something about it to them!

This showed me that the campaign was working. People were intrigued with the Painted Baby and searched to find out more. Those who knew the story were talking about it over dinner and at the golf course. Most importantly, they got it. They weren't turned off by the fact that my company wasn't 100 percent perfect 100 percent of the time. They admired that we were open and honest about those times when things went wrong too. I loved talking with that couple. They were kind and understanding. They wanted to hire a house painting company that could do a great job at a great price, but they were also interested in the character and values of the people who were doing the work. The PBS not only was different, but it also attracted the kinds of clients that we wanted to work for. As they saw this campaign directing them to take action and call us, they did so. The campaign hit on all three of Mike's pieces of the DAD framework. Mission accomplished.

The Painted Baby Story changed my business for the better. It was a turning point that made me think differently about how I interacted with clients and how I did business. I created a hypothesis around how I could use the story to continue to connect with and connect deeper with my clients, tested that hypothesis, and proved it through results. Through that entire process, I did something else. I became a storyteller. As we move into Part Two of this book, I am looking forward to helping you become a master storyteller. I am looking forward to helping you capture, craft, and communicate your Painted Baby Story.

PAINTED BABY WORKBOOK RESOURCES

Be sure to download my Painted Baby workbook. To do so, visit:

→ https://www.mattshoup.com/free-tools/

When you sign up, you will receive the workbook along with many other tools to grow your business and advance your leadership.

Don't forget to check out the Painted Baby photo shoot images here:

→ https://www.mattshoup.com/painted-baby-photo-shoot/

QUESTIONS TO CONSIDER

1. What are some different and unique marketing strategies you can implement to attempt to connect with your clients?

2. How are your current competitors advertising and messaging? What is the general practice when it comes to marketing in your industry? How can you turn left when everybody else turns right when it comes to marketing?

3. Is there anything your competition is doing to show their real side, their human side, their imperfect side? What would it look like if you began to do this in your messaging?

PART TWO

TELLING YOUR STORY

The first time I told my PBS, I kind of stumbled through it. I hadn't planned on talking about it at all, not that day—not ever. The more I retold the story to my crew and my clients, the more I realized that there's more to telling a story than just regurgitating every last detail of an event. People don't want to read or hear stories that don't apply to themselves. They want to read and hear stories that teach them something that they can then apply in their own lives. This doesn't happen by accident. There is an art, a formula, and a craft to telling a great story that connects with a person and inspires them to action. That's what we're going to talk about in these chapters.

Taking my Painted Baby Story from simply retelling the chain of events that happened that day at Mrs. Angelo's to a real story that engaged people, helped them see themselves in my story, and allowed us to connect, required three more C's. I refer to these Three C's as the Three C's of Storytelling. A great story first needs to be Captured, then Crafted, and finally Communicated.

I mentioned earlier in this book that the combination of the Three C's of Changing Your Story and the Three C's of Storytelling make up the Six C's of Brave and Vulnerable Storytelling. Let's dive into the Three C's of Storytelling so you can be ready to share your Painted Baby Story with the world.

CHAPTER 6

CAPTURE: THE PROCESS OF DISCOVERING AND BUILDING YOUR STORY

Earlier, I shared the story of Rick Scadden and the day he shared his powerful story with our leadership team. What I didn't share was the response he received from the team. There was not a dry eye in the house. There were ten full-grown adults circled around our conference table crying. Rick had perfected every detail of this story in such a way that it connected with us and hit us deep at our core. Rick's message had a purpose and intention to drive others to action (and tears). He had meticulously captured every detail of the story and why and how each detail of his story was important and would inspire the receiver of the story to action. The audience could tell that above the capturing, he had also crafted and communicated his message with excellence. When Rick finished speaking, I gave him a big hug and we stepped outside to have a chat.

"WOW," I said, "that was the best version of this story I have ever heard. Remember the first time you shared this story with me?"

"I would rather not," Rick said.

We both broke out in laughter.

"That story sucked the first time I told it," Rick exclaimed.

"It didn't suck," I replied. "It just wasn't polished enough yet. But it had to be told, and it had to be shared for the first time so that it could be shared the way it was today."

The first step in communicating a great story is capturing the details, and the essence of the story. What lesson do you want to share? Who will you share this message with? What call to action do you want them to take? How do you want this story to impact your recipient's life? In your case, you want a story that will connect with your client and build a deeper relationship with them, which will ultimately increase your business and bottom line. Keep this in mind as we move on to the exercises in this chapter.

The first time you share your story and any story for that matter, chances are it will come across like Rick's did the first time. It will be choppy, all over the place, unorganized, uninspiring, and may not lead anybody to action, thought, or your desired outcome. This was definitely the case as I began sharing my PBS more and was also the case for Rick as he continued sharing his story.

A story cannot be mastered until it is practiced and repeated over and over again. As you do so, it will continue to refine itself over time. Many people are critical of their story because it is not where it needs to be, but they fear the space they must step into to share it and refine it along the way. Because of this, many people are afraid to share a new story, or a revealing and vulnerable story at all. They fear not only being real and vulnerable, but they also fear sharing it in such a way that it actually pushes others away versus drawing them in.

There is continued discovery throughout the process of sharing your story.

As I was interviewing entrepreneurs for this book, many were excited and ready to share their Painted Baby Stories with me. They were comfortable in owning the story and had shared and experienced it enough to know how it would flow, be told, received, and most likely, how others would respond to it. For the many who were ready to share their story, I also came across a few who were reluctant to share their story and not comfortable yet making their story known. They were unsure how to tell it, and how it would be received and responded to. They had not yet captured the essence and power in their story and were fearful of judgment by others. I had a few entrepreneurs share their stories with me but asked that I not share them in this book.

For example, I recently had coffee with a friend and entrepreneur who's found great success in contracting. "Really Cool Contractor," who I introduced you to in Chapter 1, wanted to tell me his story, but he isn't ready to share it with anyone else. Despite his clean-cut appearance, admirable work ethic, and his high standing in the community, Really Cool Contractor was once homeless and living under a bridge. He's too afraid to share his story beyond his closest friends. Of course, I respect his privacy and so I changed the details of Really Cool Contractor's story and left out his name.

How about you? What are your current thoughts and feelings regarding diving in and exploring and sharing your PBS? Are you ready for the challenge?

You might be afraid to even tell it in the first place. Capturing the essence of your story is all about the process of discovery and seeking clarity. This will show you where to focus your story. During this process of discovery and seeking clarity, you must also consider the call to action you want your receiver—your reader, listener, or other audience—to take. You will work on the craft and communicate stages of building your story later. Finding your story and figuring

PAINTED BABY

out what your story is all about ensures that you're telling the right
story to the right audience for the right reasons.

THREE STEPS TO CAPTURING YOUR STORY:
DISCOVERY, CLARITY, CALL TO ACTION

Every person and every business has a Painted Baby Story. No matter how many satisfied clients and five-star reviews, how many deals
and how much revenue, somewhere among all those successes lies a
horrible failure that you'd like to forget. Odds are that someone else
knows about it. Many more people could find out about it. Maybe
your best clients. What will they think of it, hearing it from someone
else? Maybe your competitors will discover it. How will they spin it?
Wouldn't you rather tell it first, your way?

PERSONAL VERSUS PROFESSIONAL STORIES

Your Painted Baby Story may be a business story. Your Painted Baby
Story may be a personal or life story. It could be a combination of
both. Remember, your story, as you capture it, must have a purpose
to inspire your clients and those you serve to build deeper trust with
you and do business with you.

If you're struggling to capture your story, think about your business and life from the perspective of others. Look beyond your own
experiences and consider the experiences of others you serve and
connect with on a daily basis for other sources for your PBS. Ask
yourself these questions and see if they jog your memory. This is the
discovery phase, the first of the three phases of capturing your story:

1. Think about your most upset client. How did that situation arise?

2. What would your competition love to know about you or your business that could be used as ammunition against you?

3. What have you done lately that was well below your usual standards?

4. What do you not want your clients to know?

5. What's your worst *true* one-star Google review? What about it makes you want to hide it from other clients?

6. When did you drop the ball despite having every opportunity to make a client happy?

7. The local news station shows up to your business ready to share a story about business blunders, screw-ups, and mistakes. They know your story will get them ratings. What story will they share?

WHAT IF I STILL DON'T HAVE A STORY?

You might go through all these questions on your own and not come up with any viable stories. If that's the case, turn to your team and others you trust in life and business. Ask them these questions. Think back to the Johari window in Chapter 3. Your story could be something that you know but others don't. Alternatively, it could be something that you *don't* know but others do.

Continue capturing potential stories and if you get them from other people, listen carefully to how they tell you about them. They may have a different perspective on what happened that you never saw or considered.

Some of your stories might be so bad or so embarrassing that you're afraid to write them down. But write them anyway. You don't have to show them to anyone right away, or ever. But to find your Painted Baby Story, you have to get it out of your head and onto paper.

Remember, at this point, the process of capturing is not polished, proofread, or buttoned up. Think of this as a brain scan and brain dump of critical events that have occurred in your life and business. Don't worry about how you will get the information out; just get it out. We will polish, refine, and button them up in the crafting section. For now, just remember the three key elements of capturing:

1. **Discovery.** What are the key elements of your story? Who does the story affect? Just detail what happened. Consider the W's of your story: who, what, when, where, and why. The most important thing here is "What are the details?"

2. **Clarity.** Within the events of the story, what are the common themes and elements that can teach a lesson? Dig into these more. Search for and seek out themes, lessons, and anecdotes within the story. The most important thing here is "What lessons do the details hold?"

3. **Call to Action.** Where you consider what you want the receiver of your story to do. What action do you want them to take based on these lessons you have shared? What do you want your customer, the end receiver of the story, to do, think, feel, believe, and act on? The most important thing here is "How will these lessons drive the recipient to act?" and "What is that action?"

To illustrate this process, let's step through discovery, clarity, and call to action with my PBS as an example.

1. **Discovery:** M & E Painting was painting a home in Windsor, Colorado. We were very busy with work after the tornado that occurred. We were working on nine homes on one street. We had been doing excellent work on this street all spring and summer. At one home, we had frequent contact with the homeowner—a mother—and her baby. She was very friendly and interactive with the crew, frequently admiring the paint job and bringing the crew refreshments. Raul and Blas were an excellent crew, always doing quality work. Raul was the company jokester. I was overloaded in the business, doing way too much. The homeowner and her baby were out on the site, admiring the job when our paint sprayer exploded and painted Mrs. Angelo's baby. There was now a massive mess to clean up, a disaster on the job site, and a potential injury to the crew, the client, and her baby. Raul called me in a panic, screaming, freaking out, "MATTEO, I PAINT THE BABY!" I raced to the job site, discovered the mess, and gathered up the story of what happened. I checked on the crews, the customer, and the baby to assess safety and any damages. Luckily, there was only property damage. The baby and the homeowner were okay, and Blas and Raul were okay. We went into clean-up mode and triage mode, making sure everything was brought back to as it was prior to the incident. We sent the Angelos to a nice dinner, and replaced all damaged property, clothing, etc. The Angelos were completely satisfied and happy with our work. They sincerely appreciated how we handled the situation.

2. **Clarity:** I was so scared. First and foremost, is the baby okay? How the heck did this happen? I was so scared of what I would find when I arrived. There was a lot of fear underlying the story. We are a reputable company with a lot on the line. We had a lot to lose if this story got out more than it

already had, especially if it was not handled correctly. We could lose future business, we could lose the business of the Angelo's, and we could damage our reputation severely in the community for a long time. This mistake could make or break our business. One big theme here is that we were faced with our biggest challenge to date, and it happened in one of the most unusual and crazy ways. We now had the chance to show what we were made of. We now had the chance to show how we handled adversity, challenge, danger, and struggle. Our reputation and the company's integrity was on the line here, and we needed to show up in a big way. There were lots of opportunities to blame, make excuses, and find ways to avoid addressing all of the issues at hand. We dove right in and addressed the situation. When the job was completed, we were able to show our client what we were made of and where our integrity lied.

3. **Call to Action:** I want the people who hear this story to hire us and do business with us. I want our customers to trust us because they know we will show up as our best, even during our worst. I want our customers to know that "core values" are just words until they are put into action. I want customers to trust us and continue to do business with us even when things do not go perfectly. I want customers to feel good about working with us, knowing they have nothing to fear. I want customers to appreciate us and respect us for the way we approach and run our business. I want customers to say yes to us, imperfections and all.

STOP! HIT THE BRAKES

After reading this chapter, is there a story that comes to mind that could be your Painted Baby Story? If so, stop here and capture all of the details of the story. Work through the discovery, clarity, and Call to Action sections as I did above with my story.

Consider the different ways you can capture all the details of your story. You can write them in a notebook; type them on your tablet, laptop, or phone; or speak them out loud and record everything with a voice or video recording app. Just make sure to document the details in some way. Take the time to just dump all of the thoughts in your head out onto the table—paper or digitally.

As you step into the capturing process, remember that things may be and will be messy. Just dig in, search, and record the information you come up with. We will work through it together in the coming chapters. Let's move on to the phase where your story will really begin to form and take life. This is the crafting phase.

QUESTIONS TO CONSIDER

1. Have you identified your Painted Baby Story?

2. If so, what are the details? Detail the components of your discovery, clarity, and call to action.

3. If you have not, who can help you discover your PBS?

CHAPTER 7

CRAFT

In 2002, I spent my spring semester in Spain for a study abroad semester through Colorado State University. During that time, I lived with a host family and absolutely fell in love with the country's language, culture, coffee, and cuisine. I've had a love affair with Spain the past two decades, and I make sure to return to visit frequently. I enjoy sharing Spanish culture and cuisine with my stateside family and friends and do so by sharing coffee as well as one of my favorite Spanish dishes.

One of my favorite dishes from the country is paella, a traditional Spanish dish with the main ingredients consisting of rice, meat or seafood, vegetables, saffron, stock, and other spices and ingredients. Every paella chef puts their own twist on the dish, making for a variety of unique paellas as different as the people who create them. Paella originated in Valencia, and my Valencian host mom, Pepita, shared her family's authentic recipe with me while I was in Spain.

Upon returning to the states, I attempted to cook paella for the first time. The first time I followed my host mom's recipe, the dish was completely new to me. I had to follow the directions step-by-step. I went to the store and carefully purchased each ingredient. When it came to preparing the dish, I read and reread every step, measuring each ingredient precisely so I could reproduce the delicious paella. Once I could make a Valencian paella exactly like my host mom's, it was time to put my own personal twist on it. I wanted a meal that was all my own to serve to my family and friends.

Over the years, I've continued to develop my skills and I now consider myself a true paella chef. I no longer follow someone else's list of ingredients. I don't have to measure those ingredients so carefully either; I just know how much of each ingredient to put in, and I taste as I go to get it just right. Now that I'm comfortable making my own variation of paella, I have the confidence to experiment even more. Anyone for seafood paella? Vegetarian paella?

It's not enough to know and communicate the details of your story to others. You must craft it in a way that resonates with your audience. Once you know your story, it's time to put it together in a meaningful way that engages the receiver. At this point, your story is still messy. It's like having all the ingredients of a wonderful dish but not knowing what to do with them. You need a recipe.

Think of your story as a delicious dish: "capturing" is choosing and understanding the right ingredients, "crafting" is preparing them and combining them in the right order and quantities, and "communicating" is serving and delivering the dish to your recipient. After you taste your dish and after you hear the feedback of others who have tasted it, you might revisit and adjust the ingredients and the preparation, and then serve it again. Each time you continue to serve it, you will make adjustments and it will get better.

Preparing and serving a paella is like capturing, crafting, and communicating your story. In Chapter 6, you grabbed all of your ingredients. Now, it's time to carefully mix and blend them together, thus crafting your story.

LAY IT OUT

Good stories don't happen by accident, nor do they happen overnight. My PBS took time and energy. I had to go back and recraft that narrative so that I could one day present it well in a high-stakes environment. Before I could communicate my story to others, I first had to communicate it to myself, find the value in it, and craft it into more than a journal entry or blow-by-blow telling of "what happened that day." It had to say something. It had to *mean* something.

Crafting involves looking at the components you've captured and understanding how they may inspire someone to think or act differently. Think back to the components of your story from when you captured them, and what call to action you desire your receiver to have. You will now begin to shape and craft your story around that desired call to action for your receiver.

Now that you have put all your ingredients out there, you have to sift through them and find the best way to combine them. In order to begin combining them, let's discuss the elements and components of a great story. Telling your Painted Baby Story is a process that will ultimately drive the receiver of your story to action. This process involves grabbing their attention, setting the scene and context, and introducing a character that is confronted with a challenge or insinuating event. The action taken by this character to address this event or challenge typically has an impact on the character and those around them. Within this impact is a lesson for the receiver to consider and take action on.

The above process consists of the following components, which are the ingredients in the recipe of your story. These components are hook, character, environment, challenge, storyline, results, a callback, and a call to action.

HOOK

When you introduce your story, you must capture the receiver's attention immediately. Consider what part of your story will draw them in and engage them quickly. What are the first words out of your mouth that when somebody hears them, they will say: *tell me more*. That piece is the hook. A good story *must have a great hook*.

When I first started assembling my story, I captured that gut-wrenching accident that produced a massive challenge in my business: we painted a baby. When I mentioned those four words to Bill, he immediately leaned in. He was immediately engaged and wanted to hear more. He was hooked.

A hook can be shocking, thought provoking, challenging, outrageous, simple, or profound. One option for a hook is presenting an opening challenge. This could be a question that makes your receiver reconsider their perspective. Your hook can be a story, sentence, or anecdote that will immediately spark interest. Once you've sparked that initial interest, you'll have to maintain their attention throughout the story.

Here are some examples of a good opening line to a hook (you may recall them):

- I've got a dirty little secret. So do you.

- Want to hear about my first date from hell?

- When Dave woke up the morning of June 8th, 1988, he was grossly addicted to alcohol and drugs

As you consider your story and all its components, how will you create a hook to pull somebody in?

CHARACTER

Your character is the person experiencing the challenge or insinuating event within your story. The character in the story does not need to be you nor focus on you. You can have more than one character in your story, but there should be one main character, the protagonist who will deal with obstacles that challenge them. The story will be told from this person's point of view and experience. It can be told in either first person (the I format) if it was you and you are retelling the story about yourself. If the character is somebody else and you are telling the story, it will be told in the third-person format (he/she/they) as you speak about them. Many business owners I have helped through the process of discovering their Painted Baby Stories found themselves as the character in their own story. Some have also found another person as the main character. Just remember the story must inspire your client to action and inspire them towards the goals you set in relation to connecting with them.

ENVIRONMENT

You'll also need to provide your receiver with context. Share who, what, when, where, and why the events of the story are taking place. Make sure these components engage your audience. The environment helps set the stage and create the area and context in which the story takes place. The town of Windsor after the tornado, a warm summer day, Blas, Raul, Mrs. Angelo, the baby, all set the context and environment for the story to take place.

CHALLENGE AND CONFLICT

The challenge is whatever conflict or obstacle interrupts the character's life that forces them to make a decision. This challenge creates drama and intrigue and keeps the receiver of your story pulled in and wanting to hear more. As you consider your character, consider the challenge they are facing. How will this challenge affect them? What do they have riding on the line if this challenge is not addressed? How will their life improve when they address the challenge? How may their life be negatively impacted if they do not address their challenge? The challenge must be clearly stated and the impact it could have on your business must also be made clear.

When we painted Mrs. Angelo's baby, the entire future of our company was on the line. If this situation was not handled properly, we could have severely and negatively impacted our business. More importantly, the baby we painted could have been seriously injured or worse. When we were faced with our painted baby, the actions we took immediately following were what would make or break us. The way we handled this challenge would ultimately be what would draw future customers to do business with us down the road.

STORYLINE

Your storyline is the explanation of what your character does and experiences throughout the story. Throughout the storyline, you'll take your receiver through what your character did, the challenges they faced, the decisions they made, and how it concluded.

Think of your storyline as a visual storyboard where important events and experiences are laid out and detailed as you tell your story.

Your storyline takes into account how you will logically structure the explanation of your events so they make up a great story.

RESULTS AND OUTCOME

Here you share how the choices the character made led to a better (or worse) life for that character. Keep in mind that choosing not to act on a challenge is still a choice that carries repercussions.

CALL BACK

Good storytelling often includes a callback to the opening of the story. In a few sentences, explain how the results connect to the hook. How can you reconnect the lesson of the story back to the initial item that grabbed their attention?

CALL TO ACTION

As you craft your story, keep the end in mind throughout the entire crafting process. This isn't necessarily the end of what happened, but rather the lesson you want your receiver to take from it and what you want them to do with it. Whether stated or implied, your call to action should ask, inspire, encourage, or challenge your audience to do something now that they've heard your story. What do you want them to learn? What do you want them to do with that knowledge? And more importantly, what does this matter for your business? How will this story and call to action create a deeper relationship to you and your business? Remember, you began to discover and determine your call to action in the capturing section. This is where it comes back into play as you craft your story.

Now that we have reviewed the components of a great story and you begin to craft your story, let's take a look at a couple of pointers and things to consider as you journey through this process.

A WORD OF CAUTION

As you begin to craft your story and begin combining these above elements of story, beware of getting into any danger zones. Consider if you are circling around, bringing up, or including any potentially polarizing "hot topics." Topics such as politics, religion, and social issues fall into this category. Many times, the rapport and connection you have built up to this point with somebody can immediately be stripped away, reduced, or completely lost when these topics come up.

Consider where your audience is coming from. What is their story? What is their cultural background? Their political views? Will your story push them away or hit any potential hot buttons based on how you share it?

LECTURING VERSUS STORYTELLING

As you are crafting your story, begin to consider how you are going to tell it. Telling a story and giving a lecture are not the same. Sitting in a classroom listening to a lecture is sort of like reading a textbook: straight-forward and fact-filled, but unemotional.

A lecture disseminates information.

Storytelling in general inspires someone to take action.

Brave and vulnerable storytelling inspires someone to take action but also includes brutal honesty, reflection, and accountability.

Inspiration rarely comes simply from new knowledge. The receiver has to feel something. They have to experience an emotional shift that compels them to do something. Maybe that something is thinking differently or behaving differently. Maybe it's trying something completely new for the first time. Maybe it's making a lifestyle change. Whatever it is, you are more likely to spark that change with a story that has some emotional qualities and creates a bond between you and the receiver than you are with a dry "info-dump."

This book is *not* about preparing a lecture. Lectures contain many of the same components as stories, but without the motivational and inspirational benefits. There's no call to action. Think about a professor lecturing a biology class. The professor explains all the steps of how cells divide and reproduce, but there is nothing for you to do at the end of the lesson except take in the information and remember it for your test. You are not motivated to change your thinking or your life.

If I were to share my Painted Baby Story as a lecture, it would sound something like this: *I drove to the house. I saw Raul. Paint was everywhere. We cleaned up the paint and made sure the baby was okay. We paid for the ruined clothes, finished the paint project, collected our money, and went back to the office.*

Meanwhile, when I share it as a story, it sounds something closer to this: *There was black paint all over the concrete and landscape. A baby was crying and a woman was screaming. Imagine you were standing there with me, covered in the same paint. What are you thinking? What are you feeling? I'll tell you what I was feeling, and I'll tell you what I was scared of.*

They're completely different things.

CRAFTING IS CYCLICAL

Once you've crafted that first draft of your story, read it out loud to yourself. Don't think of this as the communicate stage yet. Rather, you're getting a practice run in before you distribute it more broadly.

As you tell your story, you'll first find that you learn new lessons within the story. Second, you'll find that there could be a new and better way to communicate it, and that is okay. You may take a run-through of your story to find that something you interject at the beginning is better interjected in the middle of the story. You may find that a piece of information you believed was critical to the story really isn't and can be removed. Think of this process of the run-through of your story as you cooking your paella, taking small tastes along the way, making any adjustments you feel are needed.

A great story doesn't just happen overnight. It will not be its best version the first time it is told. It may actually not be that great at all the first time it is told. We will discuss how to address this more in the next chapter. A story is shaped, molded, and crafted—not once, but continually, and sometimes with each telling. Based on what you hear from others and the feedback you give yourself, you'll recraft it again and again. This is true in storytelling—and in paella.

As I perfected my paella recipes, I received feedback on the dish from friends both stateside and from Spain, the paella homeland. In 2018, my wife and I hosted a Spanish dinner night for Día de Los Reyes, or Three Kings Day, the January 6th Spanish equivalent of Christmas that's held in celebration of the three wisemen who brought gifts to baby Jesus. I invited some of my friends from Spain who were here in Colorado for the holidays.

Standing in the kitchen, preparing my paella, several people chimed in about my ingredients and preparation. Everyone seemed to have an opinion about the type of olive oil I was using, the rice, and everything else for that matter. Finally, I asked which one of them had made paella before and surprisingly, none of them had ever actually made it. They had only eaten paella and had a lot of opinions on it.

I listened politely, but I couldn't take any of their feedback seriously. One woman did have my attention though, a woman in her eighties who stayed silent the whole time. Ana reminded me of my host mom, Pepita. She watched me the entire time but said nothing. I suspected she had made a lot of paella in her lifetime, and I was eager to hear what she had to say about mine. As I continued cooking, she continued watching quietly.

When it was finished, I served her plate first. I asked her to try it before I served it to any of my other friends. This could be my shining and defining moment of paella mastery, or it could be the end of my pursuit of paella perfection. Whatever the outcome, it was all about to happen in front of many of my Spanish friends, all here to celebrate one of their country's most important holidays. Everyone watched as Ana slowly partook in the paella. She took her first bite. No response. She took another bite. Then another. She said nothing as she continued to taste. The suspense was killing me. As I looked around, all eyes were on Ana, then back to me, and then Ana. Her few seconds of silence seemed like an eternity. Finally, the verdict was read.

"Needs a bit more salt," she said, with a wink and a hand gesture signaling to me that my paella was not just okay, but A-OK, excellent in fact, and ready to serve to her and the rest of the group.

No one else said a word.

Your story right out of the gate won't be as good as my paella was that night, nor will it ever be perfect. After much crafting, serving, and recrafting, it may just need a little more salt, more spice, or just a small tweak. But it will get to a point where it is really darned amazing. Remember, at that point, it had taken me fifteen years to where I felt comfortable serving it to a woman like Ana. Crafting is all about telling your story, getting feedback, making adjustments, manipulating the formula, reframing, and doing more practice runs. Then doing it all over again.

Food for thought: don't serve up the first version of your story to Ana.

Your story isn't static. You may find yourself returning to it as you tell it, and realize a new lesson, challenge, or key factor is drawn out that makes the story better and more impactful. You may have to recapture ideas and lessons that hadn't occurred to you and craft them back into your story. This is all part of creating and recreating something new—I did it with my PBS, I have done it with my paella recipe, and I've had to do it with this book. As you evolve as a person, as a leader, as a company, you'll want to recapture and recraft your story as your purpose and business changes. Remember that this is an ongoing process, never 100 percent complete.

Storytellers, just like authors, are continuously recrafting. Of course, there comes a time when a book must be published, a story must be communicated, and a paella must be served. That is the subject of the next chapter. Let's dive in.

FUN PAINTED BABY RESOURCES

Many people have asked me over the years to share my paella recipe with them. I recently recorded a video recipe tutorial to share my recipe. When you download my free tools, you will receive it along with the Painted Baby workbook, and many other tools to grow your business and advance your leadership. To get the tools, visit:

→ www.mattshoup.com/free-tools

QUESTIONS TO CONSIDER

1. What is your best format for crafting your PBS? Will you write it down on paper? Type it up on your laptop? Will you videotape yourself or record an audio clip telling the story? Identify one way you're going to get it out on the table.

2. Who are you writing your story for and what will they get out of it? What will you get out of telling it?

3. Revisit the key elements of a story. Come up with a couple of great hooks. Consider the other elements. Who is the main character? What is the challenge/conflict/insinuating event? Set up your environment and consider the details of the storyline. What is the resolution and call to action? How do you tie it all back to your initial hook? Just start free-flowing some ideas here.

4. Once you've established your Painted Baby Story, consider how you will take it on a trial run. Will you do it solo, or

possibly share it with somebody? If you share it with some-body, who can you trust to read or listen to your story and give you honest, critical feedback—not criticism, but sup-portive feedback intended to help you improve your story?

CHAPTER 8

COMMUNICATE

One very warm spring afternoon during my 2002 study abroad semester in Spain, I stood in the center of the Plaza de Cervantes, located in *Alcalá de Henares*. In between classes, I wanted a reprieve from the hot, Spanish afternoon. An ice cream cone seemed like the perfect solution. Just about every Spanish city has a McDonald's located somewhere in or around the city's central plaza. Back in 2002, one of those delicious, fifty-cent McDonald's ice cream cones was the perfect way to cool down.

As I entered the McDonald's, I reminded myself how much my Spanish had improved and how fluent I had become in my previous four months living there. I also realized how much I loved these ice cream cones and how frequently I found myself stopping by McDonald's for one. I could order an ice cream cone in my sleep, and I had also perfected the Spanish "th" or "lisp" as it is referred to by many. I approached the counter to order my ice cream cone and was greeted by a rather attractive young Spanish woman, who appeared to be the same age as me.

"*Dime,*" (pronounced **dee**-meh) she said, which literally means "tell me," a very typical Spanish way for somebody serving you in a restaurant to take your order.

Quick Spanish lesson. The proper way to order an ice cream cone in Spanish is to actually order a cone of ice cream or "*cono de helado*" (**koh**-noh **deh** eh-**lah**-doh). Seems simple right?

I am not sure if the young Spanish woman's attractiveness caught me off guard or if my mind just simply forgot one of the basic grammatical rules of Spanish. Whichever the case, I looked at the young woman behind the counter square in the eyes and ordered a "*coño de helado*." (Pronounced **koh**-nyo **deh** eh-**lah**-doh.)

Notice the slight difference?

She did not respond by asking me what flavor I wanted. Instead, her eyes widened, her cheeks reddened, and she took a physical step back away from the counter. She immediately placed her open hands over her mouth.

I immediately realized my mistake as her shock subsided and she began collecting herself. In Spanish, a common mark, the tilde, which is a squiggly line that sometimes appears above the letter "n," changes the pronunciation and sound of the letter "n". If the letter N in a word changes to the letter Ñ, it also changes the meaning of the word.

Instead of ordering a "cono," I had ordered a coño, pronounced *conyo*. I had asked the young woman not for an ice cream cone...

but for... an ice cream vagina.

She must have realized that Spanish wasn't my native language and that I wasn't trying to offend her or creatively ask her on a date, because she recovered quite quickly.

"Caballero," she countered, "that's going to cost you waaaaay more than fifty cents!"

While I stood there trying to come up with an appropriate response, she followed up with, "For here or to go?"

While this story is a funny, though embarrassing, anecdote, it also taught me an important lesson about communication. A minor change in wording, pronunciation, inflection, timing, and many other factors can completely alter the intended meaning of verbal communication. The same slight alteration in nonverbal cues and body language may have the same effect and outcome in terms of nonverbal communication.

Not only that, but the attitudes and experiences of the sender and receiver impact the outcome of that communication. The young woman was in a jovial mood. She had probably served many Americans and knew that we struggled with particular parts of the Spanish language. If she hadn't been so pleasant and understanding, she might have slapped me back to the United States.

At its core, communication is the action by which a person, the sender, disseminates a message to someone else, the receiver. There's a reason behind that communication—an intention. Often, the receiver makes assumptions about the message. Likewise, the sender often makes assumptions about the receiver. Whether it's a squiggly line over an "n" or something else, what we intend to communicate and what the sender hears may be two very different messages.

When you communicate, you must be clear on what you'll share, how you will share it, who you'll communicate to, why you want to do so, and what you want from them after you share. (Think back to Call to Action from the Capturing section.)

Before you communicate your story, you must identify your audience and be clear about who they are and what they want. I knew the woman at the ice cream shop wanted to know what I wanted to order, so I at least got that part right. Then you must deliver your story in a way that allows for it to be received the way you intended. Here, I failed miserably, and did so only with a small squiggly mark.

That small squiggly mark not only changed the conversation, but it also changed what I would have been served.

COMMUNICATING YOUR STORY

Putting yourself out there in the public eye is one of the realest things you can do in life. It's one thing to have a massive screw up in business. But putting that out in front of people, whether it's ten people or a hundred, and sharing your truth takes real courage and vulnerability.

The basic formula for communicating requires a sender, receiver, purpose, action, setting the stage, getting permission, considering timing, respecting boundaries, and finding a place to have the communication. Start with these basic building blocks, which I'll explain in more detail. Once you have them in place and start telling your story, you'll see how the process of capturing, crafting, and communication becomes cyclical. You'll receive feedback that will help guide you toward refining your story further for yourself and your audience.

You won't go straight from capturing and crafting your story to standing on a stage in front of dozens, or even hundreds or thousands of people. Sharing your story is a journey, and just like your business journey, it begins with a first step, just like it did with Dave Albin, Rick Scadden, Marc Mero, and Dave Sanderson. All four of these people had to start with their story and tell it somewhere.

To date, Dave Albin has shared his story around a thousand times with tens of thousands of people. However, his first time was with a small group of people in an Alcoholics Anonymous (AA) meeting in 1988. That was his first step.

To date, Rick Scadden has shared his story hundreds of times and his message has reached thousands of people. However, his first time was in 2006 with a small group of twelve young men in the county jail. That was his first step.

To date, Dave Sanderson (who I briefly mentioned in Chapter 2 and will share more about in Chapter 10) has shared his story 1,800 times to roughly 200,000 people. However, his first time was with a small youth group at his local church in 2009. That was his first step.

To date, I have shared my PBS hundreds of times to thousands of people. However, my first time was with Bill over coffee in 2011. That was my first step.

My hope, challenge, and encouragement for you is that you take that first step and share your Painted Baby Story. Don't worry about two, five, ten, or twenty years down the road and all of the people who will hear it. Just take the first step and share. Whether it is to a small group of friends over lunch, a couple of team members around your water cooler, or a few friends at the gym, just share it! So, what is your story? Who do you dream to take it to? Where will you take it first? How will it impact your clients and relationships with them? Just remember, any journey and every story begins with the first step and the first share. Let's go communicate your story!

STEP ONE: FIND YOUR RECEIVER

You've no doubt heard the question, "If a tree falls in a forest and no one is around to hear it, does it make a sound?" Likewise, if you tell a story to yourself in the mirror and no one else is around to hear it, is it really a story...or was it just a practice round?

You are the sender of your story, but your story is not complete without a receiver. The first step in the communication journey is finding someone to share your story *with*. When I say someone, I don't mean your entire office, or your entire client base, or every relative who shows up at the next family reunion. That's too many people. Start small, with a trusted friend. If you don't feel comfortable telling a friend yet, consider talking to a stranger.

I'm not kidding. The fact that they're a stranger can help reduce any pressure or fear of being judged, as you won't have to interact with them ever again. Your Uber driver, a random stranger on an airplane, somebody at the local coffee shop—pick and find a stranger who may be open to hearing your story. Of course, you will need to ask permission and set some context first. Don't just approach random people and start talking. Sometimes I will even talk to our family dog, Romeo. Seriously, he is the best receiver ever. He just sits there, staring at me, fully engaged, tail wagging and all.

Regardless of who you ask to be your audience/receiver, be sure to set expectations. Tell them how long it will take and ask them if they have time to listen, and if you have their permission to share. Also share that you will ask for feedback after (we will discuss this in Step Three).

Your first audience may not be your target audience, so keep that in mind, especially if they offer feedback that may or may not be helpful nor relatable or relevant to the audience and client base you are serving. Remember at this point, you are just getting the story out to somebody. After you've practiced a few times, reach out to someone who is your ideal receiver, and tell them your story. They will better understand the perspective of your target audience and may provide a more targeted and informative response and more helpful feedback.

Don't start by sharing your story with your intended target audience. You'll recall how that worked out with my PBS. I lost a lot of sales initially because I hadn't taken the time to fully capture the critical points of my story or craft them into a work that resonated with the receiver—my prospective clients.

Many times, when we have a moment of realization, we are hasty to jump right into sharing it. We don't consider the critical elements involved in capturing and sharing the story. We understand how it impacted us at a core, gut, and emotional level. However, we have not taken the time to process how to communicate this impact to others. This takes time.

STEP TWO: METHOD, PERMISSION, LOCATION (TIME AND PLACE)

Method: Your communication can be written or spoken. Think about how you communicate best. I speak better than I write, so I spoke this book, recorded it, and crafted it from the transcribed recordings. If you choose to share your story verbally, you can do it live or you can record the audio only, or audio and video, and then send the video to your receiver. If you prefer writing your story, you can do that in an email, a document, or a private online post.

If you're not sure how best to share your story, consider your audience. Are they readers? Or would they prefer to watch a video? Do they prefer face-to-face communication?

Permission, Time, and Place: Once you've established a method and format, set up a time to share it with your receiver. Some people work well with an informal approach, by simply asking a person, "Hey, do you mind if I tell you a quick story?" I've told some of my best stories when I had no real intention of sharing them—the opportunity just presented itself and I went for it. When you're with someone in a space where you're comfortable, you can get into a flow that makes sharing easy and natural.

Other times, a more intentional approach might work better. If you go this route, you can also set clear goals and expectations. You can say something like, "I want to take you to coffee because I have a story that I'd eventually like to present at a conference one day. Can I sit down with you and share it?" Let the receiver know how long this will take and that you will want their feedback afterward.

If you opt to tell your story in person, choose a place where you'll be comfortable speaking. Some people are very uncomfortable speaking in a setting, initially, where many other people are around, like a coffee shop or restaurant. Some people are uncomfortable speaking over the phone. For others, public speaking in front of an audience is terrifying. It can bring extreme stress and fear of judgment. Find an environment where you can feel at ease and strip away as much stress, anxiety, and fear that you may have to tell your story. As you remove stress, anxiety, and fear, you will replace it with excitement and positive anticipation to share your story. Another thing, consider the environment in which you and this person typically engage in. If you're fly-fishing buddies, don't try to sit down for a coffee. Share your story while you fly fish. Likewise, if you meet up with your friend frequently for a beer, share the story while you're out for beer. Meet where the relationship flourishes and comes naturally.

STEP THREE: REQUEST AND DEFINE FEEDBACK

Before telling a story and requesting feedback, think about what you need from your recipient. Then set the right expectations with them. Give them guidance so they know what to listen for and can then give you useful information in return that you can use to improve your story. Do this after Step Two, when you have their permission and have agreed on a time and a place to tell your story.

You can ask them for general feedback, such as their immediate emotional or "gut" reaction to your story. Ask them how your story makes them feel, and what they're thinking after hearing it. Ask them if they sensed a call to action—are they motivated to do something? Compare their responses with your intentions. Is their feedback what you expected? Were they inspired or motivated the way you thought they would be? If their responses are not what you expected, you can always recraft your story. You may also find that your story inspires them and calls them to action in a different way, and a better way than what you initially intended and expected.

Ask for targeted feedback too. Be specific. Maybe you want feedback on your voice, tone, delivery, timing, flow, or one of the critical components of telling your story. Was your recipient confused or lost during any point of your story? If so, where, and how did you lose them?

If you don't agree with the feedback, that's okay. This is not the time to argue with your receiver. Whatever they tell you, listen carefully and thank them. You can ask them for more information, but don't disagree. They are giving you their time, input, and opinion that you asked for; consider all of it valuable—even if you don't like what you hear.

Look for nonverbal feedback too: the receiver's body language and facial expressions. Many times, a nonverbal response or cue will tell you all you need to hear. Did your receiver lean in signaling interest and engagement, or did they lean back with arms crossed, signaling disengagement or disapproval? Does your receiver keep frequent eye contact and engagement with you throughout, signaling that you have their attention? Or do they frequently drift off eye contact, look at or to their phone, or bounce their eyes around?

Finally, consider the source of the feedback. Are they your target audience, the people you wrote your story for, the people who need to hear it, the people that you need to hear it?

Here are some of the things you can ask for feedback on:

- Voice, tone, timing, and delivery. Is it what you were going for?

- Did the message call your receiver to action? If so, what action?

- How did they feel after receiving your story?

- Was everything clear? Was there any confusion?

- Is there anything missing? Would another piece of information or further details make your story more impactful? If so, what would it be?

STOP! HIT THE BRAKES

You've captured and crafted your story; now it's time to communicate. If you haven't tried out your story with a trusted friend yet, you need to do that now. Put this book down, open your calendar, and look at any upcoming opportunities where you can tell your story to someone. If you don't have anything available—no get-togethers coming up—then call someone and ask them to meet up. You need to schedule it to make it happen. Do it right now. Okay, done? Let's get back to the next steps.

STEP FOUR: PRACTICE MAKES PERFECT (WELL, ALMOST PERFECT)

As you start to share your story more, you'll get comfortable telling it and evaluating the feedback so you can decide whether and how to apply that feedback in the next sharing.

What is their response when you finish your story? Do they look bored, surprised, happy, or angry? Were they crying like babies like me and my leadership team? Is this the response you expected and anticipated? Were you telling the right story to the right audience? Consider your target audience and who you are to that audience. Are you a business owner speaking to other business owners? Are you a business owner speaking to high school students interested in starting a business? Are you a business owner speaking about leadership? Business owners will likely be telling their story to their team or their clients. After telling your story enough times, you'll reach a point where you feel confident sharing it with your target audience.

Set expectations upfront, especially with your first sharing. You can say something like, "I have a story that I'd like to share with you but it's still a bit rough, so bear with me." By under-promising, you're more likely to overdeliver. If you hype the story before you tell it, your audience will have high expectations that you may not be able to meet.

If you get nervous, slow down, take a breath, and smile. Telling a story doesn't come naturally to most people, especially doing so in front of a group. It took me some time to get comfortable doing it. For me, it was like walking into the ocean, wondering when the water was going to go over my head. I had to stop worrying about getting dunked and instead take a step at a time, acclimating to the water and the waves.

Your story won't be perfect, and neither will your delivery. You will always have that perfect telling in your head that you'll compare it with. The funny thing is your audience doesn't know about that perfect story and delivery. It's in your head, so they have nothing to compare the story you're telling with. However poorly you think you're doing, you are probably doing much, much better.

When you tell your story in front of an audience, capture it and record it. Reviewing an audio or video recording allows you to evaluate your story from the audience's point of view. You will see what worked and what didn't, and then you can recraft your story with what you learn.

In addition to evaluating your story and delivery, you may also pick up on responses from your receiver that you didn't notice when you were speaking. For example, did people laugh when you expected them to laugh? Did they laugh when you did *not* expect them to? Is this good or bad?

Recording allows you to see feedback from a third-person viewpoint, versus first-person. When you are speaking, you are focusing on speaking while also running a secondary, observation program of taking in feedback and adjusting along the way. Viewing the recording afterward allows you to be 100 percent in analyzation mode, which is impossible to do while telling your story.

Take the feedback back with you, review it, and consider how much of it you are going to consider and apply as you recraft and prepare to retell your story.

AVOID THE SEVEN SINS OF STORYTELLING

When you begin to communicate your story, please keep in mind to avoid what I refer to as the "Seven Sins of Storytelling." When these sins are committed, they can and will drive participants away from connection with you.

1. **Pursuing perfection vs excellence.** When it comes to communicating your story, your goal is to show your receiver how you overcame challenge and adversity and how it displays what you are made of. Please keep in mind that you are not attempting to paint a picture of perfection; rather show your excellence in addressing your situation at hand. One of the key factors that prevent humans from connecting is the pursuit of impossible perfection. Do not continue down this path when sharing your story.

2. **Easy honesty with no vulnerability.** Being honest and being vulnerable are two very different things but many times people get them confused or use them synonymously. Have you ever shared something that was truthful and honest but in sharing so there was nothing on the line, nothing at risk, nothing to lose or be compromised when you shared it? There was no vulnerability in this honesty. Maybe it was sharing a truthful piece of information that was easy to share, was already known, or held little weight in the conversation. Keep in mind that vulnerability is the process of exposing something about yourself and your story that places you in the position to be harmed, lose something important, or be judged or viewed in a negative light. Just because you are being honest does not mean you are opening up and being vulnerable.

3. **Self-focused communication.** When you share your story with the only goal and outcome being, "What's in it for me?" This will absolutely drive connection further apart. The receiver of your story can tell when it is angled to only benefit you, the storyteller. Think of a time when somebody presented to you a story with the sole intention of benefiting them, without having any regard for you, your situation or your needs, goals, and desires.

4. **Seeing your receiver as a target or $.** To coincide with #3, when your goal and outcome is to "close" a client, or land new business rather than to build a relationship, this is another thing that will drive connection apart and put your receiver on edge. Don't get me wrong; of course you want to do business with them. But not by using some slick story to do so. Use your story to make a point, build connection, and show who you truly are and why the receiver would want to do business with you. Let business flow naturally out of that.

5. **Not looking through the lens of your receiver.** Your receiver has lived their own very unique life and views the world through their lens. It is critical when you share your story, that you understand the lens through which your receiver views the world. This is the age-old, put-yourself-in-their-shoes example. Make sure as you communicate your story that you do so understanding where your receiver has come from and what story they have experienced.

6. **Not taking the time to connect with your receiver.** Before rushing in to tell your story, be sure to build some kind of baseline connection and rapport with your receiver. Not taking the time to do this can make it seem that you either are not interested or do not care about their background and perspective. In taking the time to do this, you will also begin to understand the lens through which they view the world, so you do not commit sin #5.

7. **Not letting others in.** While you are communicating your story to your receiver, it is important that you open up and share parts of your life, your story, and your struggle. A failure to do so will stifle connection. You also cannot expect somebody else to open up into trust, connection, and vulnerability if you are not willing to.

Please keep these in mind as you begin to share your story. Remember the first step in sharing your PBS is sharing it. It will not be perfect at first. As you move through the communication process, you are bound to get frustrated. Your story takes time to communicate, build, and continue to recraft. Don't be hard on yourself as your story comes to life. Remember the most important thing: your story is nothing until you tell it. It's in limbo, waiting for an audience. Find your audience and go tell your story. It's time.

Ice cream, anyone?

QUESTIONS TO CONSIDER

1. Who are you going to tell your story to first? Who will be your practice run?

2. Why did you choose your first audience member? What is it about them that makes you want to share with them first? Schedule a time or make time during an upcoming engagement. Consider taking notes or practicing a few times before you share.

3. When will you share your story with a wider audience?

4. How will you ask your audience for feedback? How have you handled feedback from others, especially feedback you may have not wanted to hear?

5. Have you ever committed any of the seven sins of storytelling in previous story telling engagements? How could that have been prevented? How will you ensure to prevent this from happening next time?

CHAPTER 9

FEEDBACK MATTERS, BUT NOT ALL OF IT

Just like being a business owner, being an author has been a journey filled with ups and downs. In one day, one appointment, one sentence, you can go from loving your business or loving your book to absolutely hating everything about it. One minute you're excited and inspired, and the next minute, you're wallowing in the depths of despair. A lot of those feelings have to do with feedback, the feedback other people give you and the feedback that you give yourself.

The truth is, this book should have been finished six years ago, but I let other people get in my head. I listened to feedback that wasn't important from people who didn't matter to me or my business. I also had amazing people in my life, and I allowed their helpful and supportive feedback to be drowned out by the criticism. Everyone has an opinion. Many people will give you feedback. Some of that feedback is valuable and you should listen to it. Other feedback is not valuable and can be destructive, especially if you let it creep into your own inner dialogue.

CONSTRUCTIVE FEEDBACK VERSUS CRITICISM

Constructive feedback comes from a place of love and care. It's intended to uplift and elevate you. The person giving constructive feedback wants to contribute to you positively. They might even ask for permission to share their feedback with you. They have value to bring and provide. These people are careful and considerate of your emotions and how you will respond. They are thoughtful with their words and how they share them with you. They want to see you win and they are often in a good and positive place in their life. They are happy and joyful and want to share and pass that around. Their feedback has a lot to say about them. Constructive feedback will always elevate you, even when it comes as information that may challenge your beliefs or force you to reevaluate or improve your efforts.

Criticism is the opposite of constructive feedback. This feedback comes from a place of one or more negative emotions. It may come from a place of jealousy, anger, fear, or hate. Your story may have hit a touchy nerve within somebody's own life and story, making them react negatively. Criticism, many times, is a knee jerk response to being emotionally triggered and is not backed up with any type of logical thought or discussion. Many people who serve up lots of criticism are really unhappy in their own lives and want to pass that unhappiness around. Critics and their feedback says a lot about them, not you.

Communication is a back and forth, a sharing of ideas and opinions and the feedback to those ideas and opinions. Feedback, both critical and constructive, can come in the form of a reaction or a response.

Reactions tend to happen quickly and are not very well thought out. Reactions emotionally bypass and short-circuit logical thought process and decision making. They are emotionally driven, knee-jerk, and off-the-cuff words that fly out of the mouth of a receiver immediately upon receiving your message. Reactions can happen many times due to your message hitting a nerve or soft spot with a receiver. They may have been severely emotionally impacted with something from your story and those emotions take over and present.

Responses require thoughtful consideration of a communication. A response plays out when the receiver takes in whatever message they are receiving and considers it logically, and then carefully plans their feedback. Responses can take time to receive as the person preparing the response may need time to process what they have taken in. When preparing a response, it is important to consider the short-term and long-term impact these words will have on the person receiving them.

Think of the difference in reaction and response to this:

You open your email to find an email from an upset customer. In this email, not only do they bring up the issue they are unhappy about, but they also decide to attack you and your company personally. What do you typically do? Do you react or respond?

I have personally experienced this. Many times, when this occurs, I find myself slamming the keys of my laptop in a quickly crafted email filled with emotional reaction and overreaction. In the past I have sent those emails. Now, I let them sit, and come back to them a day later. One hundred percent of the time, what I wrote a day earlier is clearly a reaction not a response. Once I have had the opportunity to calm down, explore perspectives, and really think out what I want to say and the impact it will have, I will then craft a well thought out response.

When you share your story, you will receive both responses and reactions. Before you allow the feedback to affect you, consider which of the two you are receiving and the perspective of the person you are receiving it from.

When you receive feedback that's anything less than positive, consider whether it's constructive feedback or destructive criticism and if it was delivered in a reactionary or responding manner. Criticism is inevitable, and the more vulnerable you are, the greater the risk of receiving it. That criticism can hurt, but it doesn't have to be debilitating. It doesn't have to keep you from sharing more of yourself so you can learn, grow, and connect with others. Telling your PBS is important and should not be silenced. There's power in your story, for you and for the people who hear it. Despite the risk of criticism, it is important for you to get comfortable sharing it.

Constructive feedback isn't always positive. It may not be what you want to hear, but it's what you need to hear. The person providing that feedback isn't giving it to you with ill intentions, but to help you. That kind of feedback, though hard to hear, is valid and should be heard.

During the writing of this book, I shared a sample of my writing with a fellow author and friend. I asked him for his honest feedback. And he gave me just that. He gave me some very tough yet loving feedback about my writing style and voice, and how it could be adapted and improved to better connect with my audience. Truthfully, I really just wanted him to tell me how much he loved it and how amazing it was. However, he would have been doing me a disservice as a friend and fellow author if all he would have done was feed my ego. What I needed was positive, considerate, encouraging, and constructive feedback where my best interests were in mind.

DEALING WITH THE HATERS

When I was in the eighth grade, I was with a group of friends at the water park. Trying to impress my friends, I cut in front of a girl in line and said some very unkind words to her. She punched me in the face, chipping my tooth, and threw me down the waterslide. It was an important lesson that I have always remembered. This lesson taught me I am accountable for the words that I say and the words that I say have repercussions and consequences. These repercussions and consequences were looking me right in the face and were in the form of that girl's fist. I absolutely deserved what I got for saying the things I did, and I received it face-to-face.

Today, thanks to the anonymity of the internet and social media, people can say just about anything with no repercussions or accountability. And boy, can they be nasty about it. Online, you can speak to or about people directly and still maintain anonymity by hiding behind a screen. So, if the perfection culture isn't enough to scare you away from telling your truths, now you have reviewers and internet trolls to worry about. Don't let those people's actions hold you back.

My best advice for dealing with the haters is to ignore them. Like the saying goes, "Don't feed the trolls." Many of them thrive in your reaction to their nasty comments. Your reaction is what fuels them to keep going. Most of the time if you give them nothing, they will go away.

Sometimes what feels like criticism is actually constructive feedback. How do you know the difference? Say you come across a comment that hits you in the gut a little (or a lot). Before you respond, consider the source. Is this someone you know who cares about you and is calling you out from a place of caring and support? Are their comments intended to help rather than harm you? Or is the comment from an unknown source, hiding behind a screen? That person could be anyone, anywhere, and for all you know, this is how they spend their days—combing the internet looking for people to attack.

Consider every comment and don't brush all of them off immediately. When someone you trust calls you out, you know it comes from a place of care. You may also be called out by someone you don't even know, but they see something in your story that you haven't recognized, and they want to bring it to your attention in the spirit of helpfulness.

When you receive feedback, one way to determine whether to entertain it is to consider what I call the "Five Questions to Filter Feedback."

1. **Reaction vs Response.** Did the person giving the feedback take the time to properly and logically evaluate their response? Or was it a knee-jerk, emotionally driven and fueled reaction?

2. **Credibility and Relevance.** Does the person giving the feedback have any credibility and experience as to the topic they are speaking about? Are they relevant at all to the conversation or topic at hand?

3. **Anonymity.** Is the person giving the feedback willing to put a face and name to their feedback, or are they hiding behind a computer screen? Would this person consider sharing this feedback with you to your face?

4. **Do they wish to enhance and improve your life?** Were the comments and feedback made and given with the desire to truly make your life better? Is this person interested in positively contributing to your life, business, and leadership?

5. **What movie are they watching?** By this, I mean that everybody is watching a slightly different movie based on their own story and perception of the world and reality. Everybody lives in their own reality. Some people's reality has nothing to do with yours and will never relate to yours. Consider if the movie they are watching and viewing the world through is titled something along the lines of *Life is Wonderful and Amazing*, or something along the lines of *I Suck, You Suck, We All Suck: Let's Troll*.

Not everyone's comments deserve your response. If they don't check any of the five boxes, ignore their comments and move on with your life. *Don't feed the trolls.* Their comments have nothing to do with you. Their criticism really is all about *them*.

When I put my book down, I was listening to voices that didn't matter. I had to stop listening to those voices and focus on the right ones, the ones that mattered.

Not only is your PBS going to allow you to connect deeper with clients, but with others in your life and in your business. Please don't hold back from sharing it. The world needs it, and I am proud of you for planning to share it.

Remember who you are and who you've committed to be in your business, in your leadership, and in your personal journey. Focus your energy on your destiny and align with others who support, encourage, and drive you toward it. Fuel yourself with the stories of others who have done what you are doing. Learn from them and take heart from their stories, their success, their support, and their feedback.

YOU'RE PART OF THE EQUATION TOO

There's another piece to this—your voice. Many times, your own voice is stronger and more influential than the voices of others. It is important that you vet your voice through the Five Questions to Filter Feedback both when it relates to your internal voice that is *you*, speaking to and about yourself.

We all have past experiences in our lives that impacted us deeply and have become part of the base of our core memories. Many of these experiences have left us with empowering beliefs and thought patterns. Think back to a time when you experienced a massive accomplishment, goal, or dream. You achieved success and you knew it. During this moment, the "build you up" voice inside was fed, spoke to you, and continues to speak to you. You may have also had this voice fed by an encouraging parent, teacher, or someone else who mattered to you. You contribute to feeding this voice with your own internal dialogue, thought patterns, and self-talk.

Some, however, have experienced quite the opposite. Everybody has a part of their story that has left them angry, hurt, betrayed, let down, and wounded. These experiences leave behind a dirty little disempowering voice that pops up at the worst of times. This voice can and will wreak havoc within your own mind. You know what I am talking about—that inner voice that doesn't believe in you, even when everyone else does. That voice, like an old song on the radio that keeps playing, bringing up your past hurts, pains, and failures. Many times, this internal voice is louder than the external voices of Critical Clark and Tonya the Troll. That voice originates from your history and does not need to fuel your destiny. Leave it in the past— it has no place in your present or future. You will always run an internal voice and dialogue in your head, the question is, which voice will it be? Will it be the internal critic who cuts you down and focuses on the not-so-happy parts of your past? Or will it be the voice from the person you wish to become? The person you envision to be. The person you are *meant* to be. The person who others believe in.

QUESTIONS TO CONSIDER

1. To what degree have you listened to and considered voices that do not matter?

2. Think back to the last piece of impactful feedback, advice, or criticism you received. Vet it through the Five Questions to Filter Feedback. What did you learn?

3. What systems and processes can you put in place to capture both internal and external negative feedback when it arrives?

4. Take note of your own internal voice. How much of it is positive, encouraging, and uplifting? How much of it is the opposite? How often does this happen? When do these voices present themselves?

PART THREE

LIVING YOUR STORY

We've gone through a long journey together in this book. To start, I shared one of my worst days as a business owner. I told you how I overcame that challenge and shared the story, using it to build connections with clients, my team, and others. This happened only after I was called out, considered my options, and committed to change how I conducted my communication and storytelling in business, and later, in my personal life. Through this journey, I had to learn how to capture, craft, and communicate my story well.

This process was a challenging and difficult one, yet exciting and inspiring at the same time. Now I'm challenging you to do the same. As we enter into Part Three, we'll discuss why leaders have to go first and why *you* have to go first. Going first can be scary. Your gut instinct might be to come up with a lot of reasons not to share your Painted Baby Story. You may already be thinking, "Yeah, this worked for you Matt, but..." or, "This just seems so uncommon, and against the grain of what most other businesses and business leaders do."

It is completely natural and okay to be fearful, skeptical, and have doubts. Let's talk and walk through all of this together. Let's discover why, in Chapter 10, "Leaders Go First," and in Chapter 11,

let's address when you say, "Yeah, But." Chapter 12, "Painted Baby Stories," highlights other business owners who shared and owned their Painted Baby Stories, the outcomes they experienced, and lessons they learned.

As important as the lessons I learned from the PBS were to my business, there was a more valuable lesson gained through the experience, which we'll discuss in Chapter 13, "Life Is Business, Business Is Life."

CHAPTER 10

LEADERS GO FIRST

Every year, I travel to Spain for two weeks with either my daughter, Hailey, or my son, Riley. These two-week father-daughter/father-son trips give me a chance to connect with my kids without the distractions of everyday life, in a country we all love. In 2021, Hailey was ten years old, and it was her turn to hang with Dad.

She and I hit the road on a scorching hot July morning, eager to get to our next destination, the coastal city of Alicante. We had spent the night at a friend's home in Malaga, and Hailey stayed up way too late with her friend playing video games and eating sweets. She was not feeling very well the next day. We awoke early to get on the road, with a five-hour drive ahead of us. And just a few minutes into our trip, Hailey threw up. After attending to her, I told her to rest up in the back seat while I continued the drive to Alicante.

Driving along the A-7 highway with Hailey asleep in the back seat, I listened to music and soaked in the incredible views of the Mediterranean Sea. I rounded a bend and slowed down behind a long stretch of cars that began inching along the highway.

As we got closer, I saw the reason for the traffic jam: a car accident. There was a car that had obviously been involved in the collision, and a man lying on the side of the road. He was covered in blood, screaming, and waving his hands frantically. A few other vehicles stopped and pulled over, and a few bystanders stood around, but there were no emergency services on scene yet. At this point, there was nobody directly helping this man.

In the Shoup house, we have a saying: "Shoups stop to help," and this was no different. I found a safe way to pull off to the side of the road, and having recently recertified in first aid and CPR, I followed the proper protocol of checking that the scene was safe before getting out of my car. I also woke Hailey, letting her know I had to stop to help and for her to stay in the car with the AC running.

As I exited the car and approached the man, I immediately noticed his foot and ankle. It was severely mangled, twisted sideways and upside down, obviously broken. Covered in lacerations and bleeding profusely, he was screaming in a mix of English, Spanish, and Russian. His blood was pooling on the hot pavement. A young man was standing nearby, hands on his head, and clearly in shock. A young woman stood by him, crying profusely while pacing back and forth. Quickly putting two and two together, I figured out that the man on the ground had been hit by their car.

I knelt down, introduced myself to the injured man, and asked if I could help. As I was communicating with the injured man, I peered over my shoulder to see another man on scene. The man was Spanish, probably in his fifties, dressed professionally wearing suit pants and a nice button-up shirt. He was smoking a cigarette.

"Soy médico," he said. *I'm a doctor.* Then he took a puff of his cigarette.

Relieved, I asked, "Can you help?"

"I called for an ambulance," he snarked.

Then he took another puff of his cigarette, continuing to stare down at me and the injured man.

"Are you going to *help*, Doc?" I repeated. Here was a doctor—a man who by all accounts had the knowledge and authority to take charge of the situation and help the injured man on the pavement. Yet, he just stood there smoking a cigarette. Observers gathered behind him, peering at us curiously. I quickly realized I would be the one taking charge of this situation until more help arrived.

I spoke to the injured man and learned his name was Vladimir. Communication was difficult, as Russian was clearly his first language, but we were able to have a choppy conversation with a combination of English and Spanish. I wanted to keep him calm and make him as comfortable as possible until emergency services arrived.

EMS and police showed up and took control of the scene. They asked me to stay by Vladimir's side, not only for my bilingual skills, but also due to the rapport I'd built with him. Everyone else, including Dr. Cigarette, was ushered aside.

Lying there on the pavement surrounded by paramedics, Vladimir frantically began asking about and searching for his dog. Looking around, he became more and more frantic and agitated. Apparently, he and his dog had been separated in the accident. The EMTs were having a hard time working with him and he became very physically and verbally combative, due to the fear for his dog and its whereabouts.

To calm him down, I assured him not to worry—we'd find his dog. Glancing around, I finally spotted the dog under the highway barricade behind us, nestled in the shade of some bushes and thistle, no doubt in an attempt to stay cool.

I pointed to the dog and told Vladimir, "Your dog is right over there." Instead of calming down at the sight of his dog, he started yelling for it to come to him. The dog cowered deeper into the brush, obviously frightened by the scene. Here was his owner, lying on the hot pavement, surrounded by strangers and bleeding all over the place. Not to mention screaming his poor dog's name.

Instead of leaving Vladimir and going for the dog, I returned to the car and called on Hailey.

"Hailey, I need your help. There's a dog over here that needs your help. Don't look at anything else; just come over here and be with this dog."

Without hesitation, she grabbed a bottle of water and an umbrella from the back seat—shade from the midday sun—and headed for the pup. I stayed by her side, knowing she'd freak out when she saw Vladimir, and I quickly calmed her and told her she only needed to focus on the dog.

A lover of dogs, Hailey was more than happy to connect with Vladimir's dog.

"Hola perrito," she called out. *Hi puppy.* Hailey knelt down beside the dog and continued to slowly inch her way towards him with her umbrella and water bottle. As she moved closer and closer, she continued to call out to him and gauged his response. Once in close contact with the dog she gave him a pet, some more kind words, and set her umbrella up in the bushes to directly shade the dog. She poured some water into her cupped hands, and the dog immediately began to lap up the water. She giggled and continued to care for the dog. I took a few pictures with my phone.

As Hailey hung out with the dog, I re-approached Vladimir, who had now been placed on a stretcher and was being loaded into the ambulance. I assured him his dog was in good hands with Hailey. I took out my phone to show him the photos I took. He immediately breathed a sigh of relief and stuck his hand out, searching for mine to shake it. I extended my hand for a shake, and he squeezed it tightly. The ambulance pulled away, and the police recovered his dog, following the ambulance to eventually reunite the two.

Later, we learned that Vladimir was homeless. According to the driver of the car that hit him, he had run into the middle of the A-7 highway, let go of his dog's leash, crossed his hands over his chest, and stared up at the sky—an apparent suicide attempt.

As the scene cleared, I stood in awe of Hailey. This brave little ten-year-old girl, who just an hour ago threw up and then passed out in the car, bravely stepped up and into a scene filled with chaos and carnage. She was asked to help. She knew she could help. She did help. Although she was scared, she took action. Although there were difficult things occurring around her, she took action. She focused her attention on the task at hand and made a significant difference that day.

Leaders are faced with difficult, challenging, and scary tasks— sometimes on a daily basis. Being faced with sharing some of your worst, most difficult, and challenging moments in life and business is a scary thing. However, you as a leader must go first. You must step into this space of vulnerability when the time comes, and the call is made.

LEADERS PUT THEMSELVES LAST

Remember Dave Sanderson? I met Dave, of Dave Sanderson Speaks, at an Entrepreneur's Organization event in Atlantic City, New Jersey, in 2013. Four years earlier, on January 15th, 2009, Dave boarded US Airways Flight 1549 at LaGuardia airport in New York.

I promised you the rest of Dave's story, and here it is:

You may have heard of Captain Chesley Sullenberger, also known as "Sully," who successfully landed Flight 1549 in the Hudson River. What you may not know is that my friend Dave was seated as a passenger on that plane. As the plane descended, impacted the river, and immediately began to fill with icy cold water, Dave made a decision that would ultimately save countless lives that day on the Hudson.

Sitting on the plane before take-off, Dave listened closely to the safety instructions provided by the flight attendants. Unlike many passengers, Dave always listens to those instructions, and on this day, he was especially glad that he did. While ascending into the sky during takeoff, the plane impacted a flock of birds, creating a loud crashing sound. Upon hearing this loud crash on the right side of the plane, Dave realized that something was wrong, and he suspected that whatever the crash was had taken out one of the plane's engines. Captain Sully soon called over the radio instructing everybody to remain calm, to fasten their seatbelts, and that he needed to make an emergency landing. Dave still thought that just one engine was out. Little did Dave know, but the birds had actually destroyed *both* engines. He looked out the window as the plane was descending and was surprised that there was no airport in sight. New Jersey was to his right side and New York to his left side. Upon seeing this, he realized that the plane was quickly descending to its landing point, the Hudson River.

Then he heard those famous words over the plane's intercom: "Brace for impact."

The plane landed in the Hudson River, and as smooth as it appeared on the television footage that would later be viewed by millions, the landing was extremely rough. When the plane hit the water, the whole bottom of the plane was taken out and everybody was up to their knees in ice-cold Hudson River water. Dave remembered the flight attendant's instructions, and his first thought was, "I need to get off this plane."

Although people were scared, they stayed calm. They began to exit the plane in a surprisingly orderly fashion. It came time for him to get off the plane, and he thought back to something his mom told him: during times of struggle, if you do the right thing, God will take care of you.

Dave thought about this and instead of getting off the plane, he made sure everyone else was off the plane first, and he was the last one to leave. The passengers lined up on the wings and were then transferred into rescue boats. Even though he was the last one off the plane, he was the first one to get on a boat because it just happened to pull up alongside his position on the wing. It was a Red Cross boat. Dave got in, and then looked back at the other passengers as they too, were approached by boats. One passenger, a woman, was holding a baby in her arms. She appeared frozen in fear, unable to move. People tried to get her attention and get her to move, but she didn't budge.

Dave thought that the woman might be afraid to move for fear that she'd drop the infant in the water, and she probably needed both hands to get into a boat. He yelled to the woman, and she turned to look at him.

"Throw me your baby!" he said. The woman hesitated for a moment, then she threw the child and of course, he safely caught it. She ensured the child was safe, then she stepped into a rescue boat.

Dave could have just looked out for himself that day. Instead, he looked out for others. He made sure that no one was left on the plane, and he helped a mother get herself and her child to safety. Although he too was scared, and although he didn't know how the day would end for him or for any of them, he stepped up and took the necessary actions to ensure everyone's safety. He stepped further and deeper into his leadership that day.

Sometimes leading means acting and going first. Sometimes, and in Dave's case, it meant putting himself last. In both cases, there is risk involved, there is fear involved, there is uncertainty involved, there will be judgment and reaction of others involved. The greater the risk and the bigger the challenge, the more is on the line. As a business owner and leader, you have a duty and responsibility to step into this space. When it comes to your Painted Baby Story and sharing it, there will be risk involved, there will be fear involved, there will be uncertainty involved, and there will be the judgments and reactions of others involved. Stepping into this space is required in order to grow, yet many will not take this step. As we venture into this chapter together, I am challenging and encouraging you to take this step. Are you ready? Let's do it!

WHY MANY DON'T STEP UP

The term "bystander effect" refers to the phenomenon in which the greater the number of people present, the less likely people are to help a person in distress. When an emergency situation occurs, observers are more likely to take action if there are few or no other witnesses. What does all this have to do with your story? One of the core tenets of leadership is that leaders step into the unknown, step into new situations, and are willing to try new things. Many times, others around you are looking to follow. They just want to see you bravely go first.

Like approaching a chaotic and challenging scene, going first and sharing your PBS is difficult. It is scary. There are many reasons and excuses that can be stated to not go first. Standing by and waiting for someone else to go first is much easier. Many people will not take the initiative to act. Many will watch from the sidelines. They will run from, hide from, or completely ignore the calling to take action, even sometimes criticizing the person who does take action.

People are presented every day with the opportunity to step up, take action, go first, and internal voice that presents itself. One characteristic of a leader is that they listen to this voice, step up, and take action. That's what people do when they start a business, and what business people do when they step into a leadership role. If you came upon a scene like this, would you step in to help, or stand by like Dr. Cigarette? What "car accidents" are you facing in your business today that would benefit from you stepping up to act, instead of standing by? Are there any places in your business and leadership where you are being called on to put yourself last and others before you?

Maybe you're reading this and thinking to yourself: *I know I'm supposed to be a leader, but I'm afraid to go first.* On the other hand, you might think that you've got this and you're ready to go for it. You might need some help, and that's okay. I needed help at the car crash scene—from the paramedics, and from my daughter, Hailey. Being a leader and going first doesn't mean you have to do it alone. Look to others around you who will help and support you through your leadership journey and the brave steps you take within it.

BE THE FIRST TO TELL YOUR STORY

In September 2020, Mike Michalowicz reached out to me about my Painted Baby Story. He wanted to share it in his upcoming book: *Get Different: Marketing That Can't Be Ignored!* I met Mike back in 2011 after he had written his first book, *Toilet Paper Entrepreneur*. Over the years, I was always inspired by him and looked to him as a friend, role model, and mentor in the business and authorship space. Needless to say, I was absolutely honored to share my story in his book.

When *Get Different* was released in September 2021, I was ecstatic to read it. I was in Spain at the time, and I downloaded the Audible, found a comfortable spot on the beach overlooking the Mediterranean Sea, and settled in to listen.

I was so proud to hear my story. Mike did a wonderful job communicating it to his readers. Listening to it play out that day on the beach, I realized that my story had value. I then realized the power this story had, and that it was my responsibility to share it with other entrepreneurs. I immediately thought back to 2016 when I decided to put away the manuscript for *Painted Baby*. During that hot and sunny moment of clarity, I realized I should have been sharing my story. After years of picking up and putting down my manuscript, I committed right then and there to see *Painted Baby* through.

Listening to Mike's book immediately took me through the Three C's of Changing Your Story, and of changing my story. After laughing through the story with Mike, I was also immediately called out. I was called out for not finishing this book. I was called out for not fulfilling a promise I made to myself and to you, my fellow business owner.

I was also called out by Mike when I called him up to congratulate him on his book and thank him for sharing my story. When I did so, he said to me:

"Matt, you need to finish *Painted Baby*. You need to be the one to continue to share this story."

I sat for a long time on the beach that day after being called out.

I closed my eyes, listened to the waves crash, and began visioning. I played out two visions. One included me never continuing to write again and what that would look like. I then had a more powerful, purposeful, and inspiring vision that you, that's right you, were holding this book in your hand, reading it. Maybe you are on the beach somewhere listening to or reading this and committing to making some really big changes in your business and life to drive it forward toward greatness, deeper connections, and an overall better business and life. I realized that this would never happen if I did not commit, and I mean really commit. At that moment, I decided, declared, and committed to finishing *Painted Baby*.

Although I shared my story with many in Northern Colorado, Mike was the first one to take my story to the masses. I am so very grateful and thankful for this. At the same time, I should have been the first one to share the story.

Consider whose life you will *not* impact if you decide not to share your story. Who will ultimately benefit by you sharing your most real, imperfect, and unique self? How will it make their life better? Keep in mind that this book is to give you the tools to connect with clients, and in doing so, you will also connect with others that your story will inspire, uplift, and encourage. The world needs your story, and the world needs you to tell it.

Don't wait for someone else to tell your story. You go out and tell it first.

LEADERS DON'T LEAD ALONE

Listening to Dave share his experience with the Miracle on the Hudson, it's obvious that he stepped up in leadership, put himself last, and sacrificed himself to save other people. The really cool thing about Dave as a person and the way he shares this story is that he doesn't take all the credit. He acknowledges that he did not do it all alone. It took the actions of everyone on the plane working together to make sure that everyone got to safety. When Hailey and I came upon that accident, we also worked together as a team. I couldn't manage the injured man and the dog alone, and we both had to step up alongside others to ensure a positive outcome.

True leaders don't carry all the responsibility of leadership and because of that, they also don't take credit for the outcomes in the execution of that leadership. They empower others to take ownership, accountability, and action. The biggest lesson I learned from that day at the accident is that true leaders lead not by taking on all the responsibilities on their own shoulders, but by recognizing the capabilities of others around them—the paramedics, Hailey—and giving them the space and the resources to step up too.

Okay, we have arrived at the end of this chapter together. Are you ready to share your story? Are you still having doubts? I know when I am getting ready to do something big, doubt will creep into my mind. Have you ever been just ready to take a leap and the big "YEAH, BUT" creeps into your head? I know I have been there and heard that. Let's address many of the *"yeah, buts"* I have been faced with as well as those that entrepreneurs have shared with me when it comes to sharing their Painted Baby Story.

QUESTIONS TO CONSIDER

1. What have you recently been called on to do? When did you decide to step up and take action? What did that look like?

2. What about the opposite—what was something you were called to do where you decided not to do anything? What happened? Did someone else step up or step in? Take the time to give yourself an honest evaluation from one to ten on how frequently you follow through when you're called on to act.

3. Think back to a time where you were forced to take a big first step as a leader. What happened? What was the outcome? What lessons did you learn? How were others impacted?

4. Think back to a time where you were made to put yourself last as a leader. What happened? What was the outcome? What lessons did you learn? How were others impacted?

5. Do you relate to any of the reasons why people don't go first? Share examples. How can you overcome this? How have you overcome this?

CHAPTER 11

YEAH, BUT

Remember Really Cool Contractor? When I met him in 2019, he was a young and very successful contractor closing tons of business in Northern Colorado. Eight years ago, he was living under a bridge in Southern Florida selling water bottles.

Here's some more of Really Cool Contractor's story.

I met Really Cool Contractor at a local networking event in 2019. I had always admired him and his company due to his approach to marketing and his reputation in the community. Everywhere I ventured around Northern Colorado, his company grabbed my attention. His advertising was everywhere, his signs were everywhere, and I couldn't help but notice his strong social media presence.

When I met Really Cool Contractor in person, he was so full of energy and determined to succeed. We had both been so busy in our respective companies that we had never had a chance to sit down and connect. In early 2022, I sat down with Really Cool Contractor at our coffee bar, Café Sevilla. We discussed everything from life, leadership, family, and business, to—eventually—our Painted Baby Stories.

Over coffee, he shared with me something that I didn't know about him, a secret he had never shared with anyone before.

Our initial conversation circled around how he founded his

company and became successful so quickly. As we continued to share our stories, I asked him about his life before moving to Colorado to start his company. When I asked him this, he became visibly nervous and reluctant to discuss this part of his life. My interest in his story kept me asking questions around his life before contracting. As we continued to share coffee, he interrupted me, stating:

"Hey Matt, I really want to share something with you about my past, but I am not sure I should. I have never shared this with anybody, and honestly, it's scary to think about."

I shared with him that it was up to him if he wanted to share his story and informed him that I would love to hear it. After a few moments of silence, finally, he said, "Okay, I'm going to tell you this, but I'll probably never repeat it."

Then he went on to share with me the story of his life before becoming Really Cool Contractor. I leaned in to hear his story and after hearing it, I was blown away. I knew that we had connected on a deeper level than we ever could have on social media or at a typical networking event. I was impressed with his story and how he managed the adversity and challenges he faced.

I asked him why he didn't share his story with more people, and he explained a number of reasons why. In the next chapter, I will share Really Cool Contractor's story along with the Painted Baby Stories of a number of other business leaders. In searching for these stories, I reached out to many other business owners who were not ready to share their story for varying reasons. They were somewhere on the continuum between "not quite convinced" and "heck no, never going to happen." This chapter is for the leader who isn't ready to share their story yet. Let's discuss all those fears and apprehensions that are holding you back, because I've had them too. If you're ready to move forward, you can skip to Chapter 12. If you're still skeptical, worried, or afraid, this chapter is for you.

THE *YEAH, BUTS* THAT HOLD YOU BACK

The many fears and doubts that prevent you from telling your story are what I call *yeah, buts*. In this chapter, we'll cover some common *yeah, buts* shared by small business owners, as well as how to work through them. We'll talk about real-life examples that will help you overcome these fears. Some of these *yeah, buts* will combine to work together against you. The more these objections stack on top of one another, the greater the friction is going to be to allow you to jump and tell your story. Let's walk through those fears right now—all the *yeah, buts* that almost kept me from telling my PBS and that can hold you back from telling yours.

YEAH, BUT #1: FEAR OF JUDGMENT

As humans, we have a natural predisposition to run from danger and one of the greatest dangers we perceive is being judged by others. As Brené Brown mentioned in her TED Talk, humans have a deep desire to connect, yet a strong opposition to being vulnerable due to the fear of shame and judgment. Take Really Cool Contractor, for example, the contractor who was hesitant to tell me his story. He had built an amazing career and was worried that telling his Painted Baby Story would leave him open to judgment, and that judgment could tarnish his career. Many times, people are more concerned with upholding the image of who they feel they need to be rather than showing up in the world as they truly are.

When you're dealing with fear of judgment, understand that every human in the world has that same fear to some degree. In any human engagement, one person becomes vulnerable when they share something about themselves that exposes them to danger. There is a degree of faith one must step into and have when taking this risk. You have to have faith that the person you're going to be vulnerable with is not going to judge you. If they do judge you, consider this: Do you really want to do business with someone who would judge you for being vulnerable enough to trust them with your PBS? Do you want to establish a close relationship with them? Can you? Put their judgment in perspective. Think about a time you judged somebody and where that came from. It probably had nothing to do with them and everything to do with you. Keep in mind that everybody carries this fear. You may share your story and be judged. Remember why you are sharing your story and who it is for. Many times, the value of this why will outweigh any judgment you receive.

That's what I told Really Cool Contractor that day, and I'm hoping he takes the step to share his story more.

YEAH, BUT #2: MY COMPANY AND MY STORY ARE TOO SMALL OR INSIGNIFICANT

People may think they need to be the CEO of a large corporation or have a huge following to be considered a leader, and in effect, to lead. I remember thinking that my story and my business were too small when I started M & E Painting. It was literally me, Emily, and a couple of painters working out of a condo. I saw these other companies with massive teams of employees and great stories of triumph. But then I considered this: if your story connects with other people, inspires them to, as John Quincy Adams said, "dream more, learn more, do more, and become more," you are a leader.

Whether your company has two team members or 2,000, your team is looking to you to lead and guide them. It's on you to be brave, step into the unknown, and show them that there's a better way to do business and life. Don't ever doubt yourself, your company, or your story or think you're too small or your story is too insignificant to impact somebody's life.

YEAH, BUT #3: WHAT IF MY COMPETITION FINDS OUT?

In the movie *8 Mile*, up and coming white rapper B Rabbit, played by Eminem, was heading into his final rap battle of the movie. For those of you who may not have seen the movie or know what a rap battle entails, I will explain. In a rap battle, two opposing rappers come to the stage with the goal to embarrass and roast their opponent into submission, silence, or right off the stage with their raps about one another. Sounds fun, right? B Rabbit was known to choke in previous battles and knew this one would be a big one for him, especially since he had many things stacked against him and he was going up against the undefeated Papa Doc.

When Eminem started rapping, he did something brilliant. He took all of his life's embarrassment, all the ways he has failed, doesn't fit it, and all the possible ways somebody else could roast him, and he roasted himself. He went first and shared his Painted Baby Story. He then went on to severely roast his opponent Papa Doc, which sent him into silent submission.

In *8 Mile*, B Rabbit confronted and addressed one of the big fears and *yeah, buts* that we all share as entrepreneurs. What if my competition finds out? What if they come across a story or information they can use against me?

The issue with holding back your story because somebody else such as your competition could find out has a couple of issues to address. First, if your competition finds out, and then shares your story, they control the narrative, they go on the offense, and you are left reacting and playing defense to explain your side of the story they just shared. Second, your customer may be wondering why you were holding something back and why they had to hear this from somebody else. Remember a lie of omission is still a lie. Third, it puts you in a disadvantageous position strategically where you will always be fighting uphill to make up lost ground.

Now consider if you go on the offensive, take the first step, and share your PBS first. First of all, you will control the narrative. You will also be first to strike, first to share, and first to tell. Second, you will show your client that you are not afraid to share your imperfection and actually will embrace it. Third, you will be in a more advantageous position strategically in regard to how you compare to the competition you are selling against. Consider these traits to further explain what I mean.

A great company shares why they are great. An excellent and amazing company shares why they are excellent and amazing by sharing both why they are great and where they have failed. They embrace their Painted Baby Story. They also will never knock their competition such as you hear in the old saying "they knocked Chevy to sell Ford."

If and when your competition approaches the potential customer you are competing to win and shares more about your faults and less about why they are excellent and amazing, they have immediately dug themselves a hole to work out of. Be sure when you are communicating with and selling to your client that you make sure they remember that. Once you share your PBS, ask them these questions:

- Are the other companies you are meeting with as transparent and honest with you about their faults and blunders?

- How has my competition balanced their shiny marketing brochure with their Painted Baby Story?

- Did my competition spend more time telling you why they are great or why my company is not?

As you venture out into the battle to win business, remember to step up and step in just as B Rabbit did. You will leave your client thoroughly impressed and many times, your competition speechless.

YEAH, BUT #4: IF IT ISN'T BROKE, WHY FIX IT?

You know that feeling when business is going not just well but going great? Things seem to be going so smoothly and well that you do not want to do anything to rock the boat, muddy the waters, or shake things up. In both life and business, you may have heard the saying: "If it ain't broke, don't try to fix it."

This is another *yeah, but* that I have run into with entrepreneurs when I have shared my Painted Baby Story with them. They explain to me that they are happy with their conversion rate, capture rate, and metrics, as well as relationships in their business. The fear that disturbing this in any way, shape, or form will move the dial backwards in their business.

Here is something to consider: It will never be better until you work to make it better.

I know the feeling of everything going smoothly in business. I completely understand the fear of sharking things up and possibly moving things backwards. Your business will not improve until you work to improve it. Many times, the idea and approach to leave things as they are because they are working and have always worked can lead to complacency and lack of innovation. When these two things happen, your business can slowly begin to decline away from its greatness.

I've mentioned Mike Michalowicz already in this book, and one of the reasons I admire him is his scientific approach to business. He's always guessing, checking, measuring, analyzing, and looking at new ways to tweak, improve, and expand his business. He is always willing to try new things and never settles for the status quo.

When I told Bill my PBS, business *was* going well. I was making money. I didn't have to change anything in order to stay the course and reap benefits. What I didn't realize until I started sharing the Painted Baby Story was how hard I was working to uphold that picture of perfection. I always felt like I was hiding something. I had to consider the effort I was putting in to try to uphold that pristine image. I also was shortchanging myself, holding myself back from rich and deep connections.

When I stepped outside of it, I realized that I could generate the same leads without putting on a farce. Not only that, but I experienced less friction. It was less struggling, working, scratching, and fighting. I never would have discovered this if I settled into the mindset of complacency and unwillingness to try something new.

YEAH, BUT #5: WE HAVE ALWAYS DONE THINGS THIS WAY

We tend to have a natural aversion to testing things because we get settled in our own ways. Humans are creatures of habit, and that extends to business. We wake up at the same time, have the same coffee, and make the same meals. Just as your morning routine is a habit, your marketing, messaging, and storytelling in business is *also* habitual. There's comfort in predictability. The flip side of this coin is that until you consciously choose to break that habit and try something new, you simply won't.

Consider your morning routine, habits, and patterns. Evaluate your last twenty-four hours of life, from the moment you woke up until you went to sleep. Maybe you have a morning routine, maybe you go to the gym, maybe you grab a morning coffee. Chances are, you're putting the same leg in your pants first, strapping your seatbelt on the exact same way every time, and driving the same morning route.

If you're anything like me, you've read a lot about how to improve your life, business, and leadership. Part of that work includes breaking bad habits and wiring new ones. Take stock of habits you've developed and ask yourself whether they are driving you forward or pulling you away from where you want to be. If you find that any of your marketing, messaging, or business habits may be inhibiting your potential for growth and connection with others, make a commitment to change them. Think back to the Three C's and how you can process your habits through this framework.

YEAH, BUT #6: I JUST DON'T HAVE A PAINTED BABY BUSINESS STORY

I told you about Dave Albin with Firewalk Adventures. He shared his personal story, and I shared it with you. I reached back out to Dave and asked if he had a business-related Painted Baby Story—something around firewalking, board-breaking, or stepping across glass. He replied, "No, Matt, that would be a *very* bad day at the office."

His response made me realize that you don't have to have a Painted Baby "Business" Story to create connections and build trust. Your personal story also allows you to connect with clients. Rick Scadden did this, so did Dave Albin, so did Terri Coomer. As we venture into Chapter 12, you will meet some other entrepreneurs who will share their PBS. Some will be business-related, and some will be personal. Remember, your story is a way to show your clients more of who you are and how you handle adversity, imperfection, and challenges. Whether they happen in business, personally, or both, your character will shine through into business either way.

YEAH, BUT #7: THIS WILL AFFECT MY PERFECT RATING

Many business owners are scared to receive a less than perfect review online. Have you experienced the not-so-perfect review yet on Google or social media? If so, you may recall the feeling of being punched in the gut, and the wind being knocked out of your sails. I recall the first day I received a negative review online and the feelings and fears that came with it.

The reality of business is that a day will arrive when your company's perfect rating will become not perfect. There are a couple of things to consider and remember when it comes to this topic.

First, this is a good thing. Own it. You are not perfect, and neither is your company. This is okay, and it is okay to have this represented for all to see.

Second, your company's online rating is not a true reflection of how well your company has done or how well it has served its clients. Your company's online rating is a reflection of how well you have served the people who decided to write reviews. Not everybody you do business with will write a review. There is no way to have everybody you do business with write you a review.

Third, a negative review is one of the best things for your company. It is also the best way you can show others what you are really made of. Most people who read reviews, especially negative ones, understand they come from one of two places. One, they are fake troll reviews, and it is clear the person never did business with said company. Two, they are a real review with a real customer who has/had a real problem with said company.

Whatever the case, reply to the review. How you decide to reply to the troll reviews that have never really done business with you is up to you; just make sure it is a reflection of your company, its character, culture, and core values. I have seen all different types of responses anywhere from none at all to dry and serious to downright comical and hilarious. People will see and feel this.

In the case that you have an upset customer, this is a wonderful opportunity to make things right publicly. Somebody who brings a concern to a public forum should expect a public response. Again, here ensure you respond as to the best way to reflect your company, its character, culture, and core values. The public will see this, and many times will make decisions about whether they do business with you based on how you respond, not what you necessarily respond to.

The way a review is written speaks much about the person who wrote the review. And the way you respond and address the review speaks even greater volumes to who you are as the business owner.

Lastly, I have never experienced a negative review being written about me due to the fact that I shared my Painted Baby Story. Instead, by sharing my story, it leaves the door more open between me and my customer to have an open dialogue if they have a true concern. Many times, sharing my PBS has prevented an upset customer from going online because they know they can come speak to me directly.

YEAH, BUT #8: NOBODY ELSE IS DOING IT

When I founded M & E Painting, I had to quickly establish a marketing method and mix that generated a consistent lead flow. I did what most business owners do: R&D, which stands for "Rip Off and Duplicate." I looked to see what other painters were doing and then I did it as well. At the time, painters advertised in the phone book and dropped door hangers and plastered signs in neighborhoods. So that's what I did.

Now, this produced me results, but I quickly became just another similar message in the sea of messages all trying to attract the same clients. Remember Mike Michalowicz's book *Get Different* where he states that for your marketing to succeed you do not need to be the best, just different. What I should have been doing was to look to what my competition was doing and then do the extreme opposite.

A few years into business, I continually drove past a man dressed up as the Statue of Liberty, waving a sign for a tax service company on a busy street intersection. At the time, no one else was advertising this way, and plenty of people were skeptical. I thought to myself, *Nobody else is doing that. Who's going to pay attention to some guy dancing around on a street corner? Who is going to take whatever he's advertising seriously?*

I asked myself a different question that I invite you to consider as well: *I wonder what could happen if I try this?*

The next week, I hired a high school kid named Ben to dance around and spin a sign for two hours. My wife, Emily, was so busy answering phone calls during those two hours that she called me to ask what was happening. She mentioned the phone rarely rang during these times and people were now calling non-stop. As she asked each caller how they heard of us, they all replied how much they enjoyed seeing the "dancing man" and how it caught their attention so much. At the end of this trial week, we received thirty-seven estimate calls from paying Ben for ten hours of sign spinning—that came out to an advertising spend of $3 per estimate.

When it comes to being vulnerable and sharing our truth, the truth that we are not a perfect company, look at the current business landscape. Not many are doing it. Just as my competitors were marketing by phone booking, flyer dropping, and sign plastering, your competitors are marketing and messaging with the theme of attempting to paint a picture of perfection.

Now is your time to do something out of the box, do something nobody is doing, do something different.

YEAH, BUT #9: I'M JUST PLAIN SCARED

Truth be told, there will be fear and uncertainty when you take the leap and share your story for the first time. It is a very natural and human quality to be fearful, especially of things that may be perceived to cause us harm, many times those things being the unknown.

FAITH OVER FEAR, TRUST OVER DOUBT

Going first doesn't have to be a grand gesture or major event. It can be as simple as trying a new marketing campaign. It's stepping over the threshold of fear into faith and action. It's having the bravery to do what others will not. This is where you will differentiate yourself, earn respect and admiration, and forge a path for others to follow.

When a defining moment approaches you, there will always be some level of fear or doubt. You wouldn't be human if you weren't questioning some of the ideas I'm presenting to you in this book. You're probably excited and motivated, but also a bit scared. You're finding logical explanations for why you shouldn't do this. Truthfully, I'm proud of you for asking those questions because it means you're human. If you had no fear, trepidation, or anxiety as you prepared to share your story, I would be concerned that you hadn't fully received the message of this book. Everyone I've shared this framework with has been nervous at one time or another.

The truth of the human condition is that we are either driven by fear and doubt or faith and trust, many times a combination of both. I hope my Painted Baby journey gives you faith over fear and trust over doubt.

Don't shortchange yourself. If you're a business owner, you've already taken a leap of faith in the past. You've already trusted yourself despite the odds. Maybe you mortgaged your house or took out a loan to start your business. You might have jumped ship from a secure position. You might have been told by those around you to quit the business early on, when you were working too many hours and struggling for traction. Think back to all the pivotal moments you have been faced with where you continued to step into faith, take action, and drive forward with your business. Sharing your Painted Baby Story is the exact same moment.

Allow yourself to take this leap of faith so you can share your PBS. All the *yeah, buts* (and the *what ifs* too), come from a source. Either someone else is sowing doubt in your mind, or you're doing it yourself (remember back to Chapter 9: Feedback Matters, But Not All of It). As a leader, you will hear all of the voices, but you get to decide which voices you actually *listen* to.

There will naturally be fear and hesitation when it comes time to take a risk and step into the unknown. I hope this chapter has addressed many of the fears and concerns that you may have. As we head into Chapter 12, I'm very excited to share with you the Painted Baby Stories of three brave entrepreneurs and what happened when they decided to share their stories as well as how it made their businesses better.

QUESTIONS TO CONSIDER

1. Which one of these *yeah, buts* do you most relate to? Why?

2. How is the *yeah, but* that you most relate to preventing you from sharing your Painted Baby Story?

3. Are there any *yeah, buts* you are facing that have not been addressed in this chapter? If so, explain.

CHAPTER 12

PAINTED BABY STORIES

This chapter by far has been one of my favorites of the book. Up to this point, we have revisited my Painted Baby Story and the observations I have made from it. I have done my best to consolidate these observations into tangible learning points that you can apply to your business. As I ventured out over the past decade and shared my PBS, many business owners reciprocated and shared theirs. I have learned a lot of lessons and have taken valuable insight from each one of these business owners whose stories I am about to share. Each one of these stories will highlight the bravery and vulnerability of the entrepreneur who shared their story. Each story will also share additional lessons and perspectives about how to handle your worst moments, what you can learn from them, and most importantly, how it makes your business better.

I hope these stories inspire you not only to share your PBS but also to see how these business owners sharing their stories ultimately improved their business and life. Some of these stories are funny, some scary, and some are downright crazy. Enjoy them!

TERRI COOMER WITH LIVE, LOVE & LAUGH HOMECARE

You've already met Terri Coomer, the former CEO and owner of Live, Love & Laugh Homecare. I told you about the challenges she overcame growing up and how she and her wife went on to sell their very successful business and retire. But what I'd love to do right now is share her Painted Baby Story.

Terri's business involved providing home care to people with dementia and many of the issues that can accompany the aging process. Her company was a lifeline for these people and their families, and Terri and her staff consistently found themselves providing care for them at the drop of a hat, around the clock.

Terri had established a deep relationship with a very well-known member of the community and was caring for one of their family members. A male member of the family was suffering from dementia and his wife was having a lot of difficulty caring for him. Terri provided the family with care for four years up until his passing. One of her caregivers showed up daily to help the man dress, cook for and feed him, and made sure he took his medications as well as provided any other daily help the man needed. She also picked up and cleaned the house, so she knew every room, every corner, every nook and cranny of the house.

One thing that Terri prided herself on was that all of her employees were given thorough background checks. In addition to checking for criminal activity, she checked their credit history, employment history, and did a deep and thorough personal reference background check. Needless to say, if one of Terri's team members showed up, you knew you were in good, hard-working, honest hands, or so Terri thought.

One day, Terri received a phone call from the wife of the man they were providing care for. She frantically explained that she came home after running errands and discovered that $360 was missing from an envelope that she kept in a dresser drawer in their bedroom. She had a thousand dollars placed in the envelope as emergency cash. On top of that she knew how many bills of each denomination were in the envelope. In the past, one thousand dollars hadn't been a lot of money to the couple. But with the man's sudden ailments and inability to work, they were feeling the weight of the lost income, not to mention the rising expenses and medical bills. The woman was very upset about the missing cash and as much as she hated to state it, she feared it was Terri's employee who had taken the money.

Upon hearing the news, Terri was in shock and disbelief. She felt awful for this couple. She knew how hard they worked all their lives and understood the frustration their family was currently experiencing. Terri was there to make life easier and more peaceful for this family and at this moment, the exact opposite was occurring. Above and beyond this shock, Terri's emotions quickly began to turn to anger, as she could not imagine why one of her trusted team members would steal from this family.

Terri had two options at this point. One would be to ignore, deny, and 100 percent back her employee. Option two would be to investigate and explore the story, and that is exactly what she did. What Terri did next was both creative, bold, and brave. She set up a sting. Terri knew that if somebody stole something and got away with it, they would most likely do so again. First, Terri immediately gave her client $360 to replace the money that was stolen. Both Terri and the client then went to the dresser drawer where the envelope was located and ensured it was left just as it was left when it was robbed.

Terri said nothing to her employee, and nothing to the husband they were caring for. They let the envelope sit and wait.

Just as Terri and her client suspected, two days later, after Terri's employee finished her shift, the wife opened the dresser drawer this time to discover the remaining $640 was gone. At this moment, it was 100 percent clear and without doubt that Terri's employee had stolen the money.

Terri immediately took action and called local law enforcement. She didn't want to tip off her employee, so Terri waited until the next day, as she was leaving the couple's home, to confront her. Terri and a police officer confronted her employee, who immediately denied being involved. Terri pressed further, explaining that she knew the exact amount of money the employee had stolen and the denominations of the bills. The police officer searched the employee's car to discover the entire stolen $1,000 in her glove box. She was arrested on the spot, fired immediately, and Terri's client decided to press charges.

Terri spent a lot of time with her client, first asking her for forgiveness and ensuring that their relationship was not at risk of being damaged or ruined. Her client stated that she was very impressed with how Terri took action, investigated, and once determined the truth, held her employee accountable.

I asked Terri to share with other entrepreneurs the lessons she took away from this story. She shared this with me.

It was so important to me, when this incident occurred, that I first recognized the severity of the situation. There was a lot on the line here. We had established a deep and positive relationship with this family, and it was now at risk of being damaged. The next thing for me to do was to take ownership and action. I immediately got to work to create both a temporary solution to the problem and the follow-up investigation/sting to get to the bottom of what happened. And once my fears were confirmed, I knew what the right decision was, and I made it.

Throughout the process, things were stressful, challenging, and many times I felt overwhelmed. Throughout, I thought back to why we exist as a company and what our mission was. Everything I did surrounding this situation was to adhere to and uphold our mission. I encourage entrepreneurs to face situations like this, as big and scary as they may be, to act fast, take ownership, and make the right decisions. The biggest thing to make sure to do is follow up with your client repeatedly to ensure things are okay moving forward.

I then asked Terri when she began to share this story how it impacted her business. She shared this.

At first, I kept the story to myself, fearful to share it, feeling a bit ashamed and embarrassed that this happened on my watch. I was asked by a client one day how they knew they could trust me. That was when I decided to share my story for the first time.

The potential client explained that there was no way she could be 100 percent sure she could trust Terri. Then Terri explained what she did and how she responded to a situation where trust and confidence were almost shattered. She explained the steps of how she engaged with her client and what she did to get to the bottom of things and make things right. She wanted her potential client to know what could go and has gone wrong and what Terri did about it. In this situation, her potential client responded that she already had a deep sense of trust and connection with Terri and this story just solidified it even more. This potential client turned into a new client for Terri.

CHRIS BRUNO WITH RESTORATION PROJECT

Chris Bruno is the CEO of Restoration Project, a faith-based non-profit he co-founded in 2010 to help men restore relationships with their families and each other. Chris does not have a degree in business or nonprofit leadership, and had come from the mission field, building missionary teams in Turkey.

Chris was very successful in building mission teams. This process involved training and educating his missionaries as to the culture they would be working in, as well as the theological content they would be sharing with others. While overseas, he worked for a large, fifty-year-old international organization with over 25,000 employees around the world. Naturally, all the organizational structure already existed when he joined the team, allowing Chris to focus his efforts on building the team, not the organization.

Starting a new nonprofit, however, required organizational vision, structure, financials, and overall direction Chris was unprepared for.

Focusing on the mission, vision, and work of the nonprofit took Chris's complete energy, and he made assumptions that others in the organization were tending to the financial management. This was his big mistake. One day he received a call from his accountant informing him the most recent payroll had overdrawn their account, and they had no money left to pay the upcoming bills. Despite having a solid foundation of donors as well as positive revenue from experiences, he did not adequately predict or manage the issue of cash flow, leaving the entire organization in jeopardy.

Chris quickly gathered the team and explained the financial situation and how arriving to it was completely Chris's fault. He consulted his board, a business coach, and several other nonprofit leaders, seeking the wisdom and experience he realized he did not have. He then detailed exactly how he planned to get back on track moving forward. His team was very understanding.

I asked Chris to share with other entrepreneurs the lessons he took away from this story. He shared this with me.

First off, this Painted Baby Story was the wakeup call I needed to hear to begin to get things back on track. Many times, in life and business, we need a situation to call our attention by screaming at us. I had been lightly nudged as to my lack of leadership but never really picked up the message others were putting out towards me. When my accountant called me with this news, it was as if this issue was being screamed across the room; it finally spoke loud and clearly to me. I would encourage entrepreneurs to listen to the soft voices that speak to us before they become loud voices. I would also encourage entrepreneurs to take immediate action when they realize they have an issue to address. In this instance, I realized there was a serious issue and I stepped in to address it.

A big lesson I learned was that bringing past experiences or frameworks in how to run other organizations or groups may not apply to business. When I was in mission work, there was a system and protocol that was followed, and it worked well in the mission field. This system did not translate into the business we were in.

My last piece of advice is to ask for help. Being an entrepreneur as well as counseling them, I have observed that we can be hard-headed when it comes to asking for help. We would rather figure things out the hard way as long as they are our way. Our pride and ego can get in the way and many times, this hinders our business and our ability to lead. As soon as I asked for help and opened the door for others, they were waiting right there to assist.

Chris began sharing his Painted Baby Story with incoming staff members at Restoration Project. Here's what he told me:

In our organization, we are meeting people at very vulnerable places and spaces in their life journey. When I, as a counselor, can share experiences from both my personal life and business where I have screwed up, it helps me to be more relatable to the person I am working with. In being more relatable, it opens up my client to share more, share deeper, and just plain be more comfortable talking with me. Things end up feeling more like two normal guys just talking through life and figuring things out together instead of the client coming to the all-knowing mighty counselor.

Not only does this transparency build deeper trust, it has also built deeper trust and connection between the team internally. Just a few weeks ago, one of our staff members made a pretty big mistake. He owned it immediately, and then proceeded to correct the issue at hand. We all joked that we had come a long way from the old days when that mistake would have run the entire ship aground.

Lastly, I have seen that sharing our Painted Baby Story shows the maturity of our organization. I have worked with a lot of leaders running organizations and their issues unfortunately flow into their organization. Lack of ability to take ownership and accountability is many times a reflection of the leader, their maturity, and the maturity (or lack thereof) of the organization.

REALLY COOL CONTRACTOR

Remember Really Cool Contractor? Here is what he shared with me over coffee.

Before I moved to Colorado, I lived in Southern Florida. I dropped out of high school in tenth grade. I was running with the wrong crowd, making poor decisions, and still to this day can't believe I didn't end up in prison. I left a very abusive home and figured it was better for me to bounce around friends' houses and couches than it was to live at home. However, these friends were into very dangerous and illegal activities, so I ultimately made the decision to leave this environment and live on the streets.

I didn't know what to do. I needed to eat, and I needed a place to sleep. I ended up living under a bridge and selling bottles of water to cars at a busy intersection.

After about six months of doing this, things took a turn for me.

One early morning in 2008, I was hustling away selling water bottles. Most of the people I sold water to were people in cars briefly stopped at the red light of a busy intersection. My conversations were very limited with them, and very transactional. Many would thank me, tell me to have a nice day, and then drive off when the light turned green. This morning, a very successful looking man, not much older than me, pulled up to the intersection in a very nice Mercedes. He rolled his window down to signal me to the car.

He asked for a bottle of water and then handed me $20 stating, "Keep the change." I was prompted at this moment not only to thank him but also to ask him how he had become so successful. When I asked this, the light turned green. He looked at me stating "I gotta go. Meet me over at the gas station." He signaled over to the gas station across the street. I watched him drive his car over and park. I ran over as quickly as I could. He exited his car, introduced himself to me. "Hey, I'm Rob." Rob asked if he could buy me a coffee. I accepted. He escorted me into the gas station and told me to get whatever I wanted, food included.

What happened after that was so life-changing for me. Not only did he invest around $30 of his hard-earned money in me, but he then spent close to an hour with me, leaned up against his car asking me about life and how I ended up where I was. As I shared my story, I also began to ask him questions about his success. This is what he shared with me that changed my life.

He said:

"My life both professionally and personally is a combination of the decisions I made and the people I associated with. You are here selling water bottles because of this. And I share this not to bring you down, but to build you up and inspire you. Just like you arrived here due to your choices and associations with others, you too can pull yourself up and out of here by the choices you make from here on out. I have passed by you every day for weeks and see you out here working. I can tell you have work ethic. I truly believe that if you continue to make good choices and associate with others who can build you up, you will be successful."

Rob then gave me the opportunity to meet with some other successful people. He invited me to a local business owner's breakfast that happened every Tuesday morning. I attended, and in doing so, met many amazing people, one of whom was a contractor named Spencer. As we got to know each other, Spencer offered me a job as a laborer to help out with small projects on his job sites. I worked for Spencer for two years. During these two years, I mentioned to Spencer I would love to own my own business one day. Spencer agreed he would show me the ways of the business in the hopes that I would spread my wings and fly one day.

I mentioned to Spencer my dreams of someday moving to Colorado. It turned out that Spencer had some connections in the Northern Colorado area, and he then introduced me to these people. In 2011, Spencer came to me and told me he believed I was ready to take my leap and move to Colorado. A couple of weeks later, I packed all my belongings and made the move. Within six months of landing in Colorado, I had established my company, landed numerous contracts, and had created some financial stability.

One year later, my business really began to take off. The rest is history!

After giving him a huge congratulations and high five, I encouraged him to keep telling his story. I asked him what lessons he took away from this story. He shared this with me:

Your past does not define you. You can change your path if you decide to focus on where you want to go, not wallow in where you have been. I realized how much my mindset played a role in my transformation. When I was under that bridge, I was scared, alone, defeated, and hopeless. I let those feelings sink in and settle within my mind and heart very deeply. Rob saved my life that day, and the words he shared with me still ring true to me to this day. I am a product of the decisions I make and the people I spend time with. I live by those words. Looking back, I also realize that many opportunities will present themselves to you. Taking advantage of and exploring those opportunities open the door to success. Both Rob and Spencer offered me opportunities. It was up to me to take them on. If I had not taken Rob up on his offer to attend breakfast meetings, I never would have met Spencer.

Really Cool Contractor had never shared his story with anybody up until our coffee meeting. At the end of it, I asked him how he now felt about making this part of his life and story more known and he shared this with me.

Matt, I am so glad you pushed me a little today to share more with you. I was always very nervous about how others would react to my past life. Opening up to you and sharing today, then seeing your response was very inspiring to me. I realized that my story has the power to help others. I think I am going to share it more.

And I hope Really Cool Contractor decides to share his story more as well.

ÁNGEL FUENTES MORENO WITH
CERAMICAS SEVILLA

Ángel Fuentes Moreno is a great friend of mine. I had the pleasure of meeting him years ago as Emily and I were wandering the streets of Seville, Spain. We met Ángel when we walked into his art store, Ceramicas Sevilla. Seville is a city known for its passion and history with ceramics and Ángel comes from a family with deep roots in ceramics fabricating and dealing. He grew up in the business watching both his mother and father collecting, restoring, and reselling ceramics recovered from buildings that were being demolished or renovated. They also manufactured hand-painted ceramics that they sold directly to customers as well as supply to other stores.

Growing up, Ángel knew the business would be passed to him one day. He now is teaching the business to his two children, Ángel and Juana, so that one day he can pass it along to them.

Ceramics are popular souvenirs among tourists visiting Seville. During the late 1970s and early '80s, ceramics shops were discovered thanks to the help of tour guides. The guides would take a group of tourists on a historical tour of Seville. They would visit a tapas bar, a flamenco show, a wine tasting, and then shopping, where they would inevitably end up at Ángel's store. The tour guides received a kickback for bringing tourists to Ángel's and other business owners' stores in the form of a percentage of sales.

The relationship that these tour guides built with shop owners was initially mutually beneficial. The tour guides would keep business flowing to the shops and shop owners were happy to compensate the tour guides for their efforts. However, tour guides began to slowly increase their "finder's fee." Ángel recalls one day asking one of the tour guides why these fees kept going up, and he was told: "We can charge you whatever we want, and you will happily pay it. Without us, your stores would not survive."

What started out as a really good business arrangement slowly turned into tour guides shaking down shop owners in a very mafia-like fashion. Shop owners who questioned the tour guides, their fees, and their practices, would all of a sudden find themselves with no clients stopping by from these tours. The tour guide mafia was running the tourism business and Ángel found himself in a very difficult situation.

He had started out paying them 7 percent of sales, but they raised their fee to 10 percent, then 15 percent, and then 20 percent of sales. As the increases continued, so did the dwindling of Ángel's profits. There was no way he could sustain and stay in business with this type of business model. However, there was no other way to do business at the time and anybody who would stand up to the tour guides would soon find themselves out of business.

Ángel had become more and more vocal about fighting back against the tour guides, first encouraging other shop owners to stop paying the finder's fees. When a couple of shop owners decided to band together to do so, they quickly found themselves without business. Ángel watched as a couple of his friends went out of business. Ángel still continued to speak up and speak louder.

One morning, Ángel arrived to open up his shop to find two men waiting for him with a message. They explained to him that if he kept "encouraging others to make life hard for us (us meaning the tour guides), we will make life really hard for you. We have no problem opening up a shop three doors down from you and sending all OUR clients to OUR shop."

Ángel realized these guys meant business and he had to find

another approach and another way to go about his business. He spent the coming weeks spending much time with his parents pondering and exploring solutions. His parents and their experience and wisdom were monumental in the solution they came up with. As they explored the issue at hand, they realized the solution to his problem was literally hidden inside the problem.

Ángel's store was located in an area of Seville where ceramics and touristy type shops were a dime a dozen. He realized he unfortunately was at the mercy of the tour guides, and they could easily funnel tourists somewhere else. He also knew that these dime-a-dozen shops all sold the same stuff, cheap junk that was manufactured overseas and shipped into Seville.

Ángel and his family were the only ones producing and selling authentic Sevillian ceramics, but the tourists didn't know it and were not necessarily looking for it. Most of them wanted a cheap trinket or gift to help them remember their time in Seville. He knew that whether he was there or not, tourists would keep buying these items and tour guides would still have their hands in the business.

Ángel and his family decided to make a big move and take a big risk. They discussed the fact that unsuspecting and uneducated tourists were not their ideal customer. They discussed that their ideal customer was a more upscale type of tourist who came to Seville searching for authentic experiences and products. They came to realize that these types of customers did not shop anywhere near the touristy shops.

His family purchased a building on Calle Sierpes, a well-known street in a bustling commercial shopping district in Seville. Calle Sierpes was known for having high-end stores and high-end brands with a high-end clientele to match. These people were not looking for a cheap trinket. They were looking for exactly what Ángel and his family were offering. Better yet, the tour guides had not inhabited and infected this area.

As Ángel and his family were nearing the date to close on their new building and move, one of the tour guides stopped by to harass Ángel a little more. He then mentioned to Ángel that the commissions would again be going up next month. Ángel informed the tour guide that his store would not be there next month. He informed them that he had found a better location and better business model that no longer involved them. He then informed them that if they wanted to open up their shop they could do so at this location.

Ceramics Sevilla set up on Calle Sierpes and business was booming. All the other cheap trinket shops were battling with and being shaken down by tour guides. Ángel and his company flourished from the 1980s into the '90s and 2000s, and the business still exists and flourishes today. I am sure happy Ángel decided to take this risk and make this change with his business, as he has become one of my very best friends in Spain.

I asked Ángel to share with other entrepreneurs the lessons he took away from this story. He shared this with me.

First, when you realize you have a problem, you better act on it. I knew these guys were becoming more and more of an issue for me, and that we were nearing a critical point of our relationship where action would need to be taken. Whatever you do, don't ignore, deny, or dance around the issue; address and attack it head on.

When we are faced with a problem as business owners, many times the solution lies right within the problem. Many times, we look too far away as business owners for a solution, when something could be right under our nose. I realized in this case that the solution to my problem with my business model was my business model itself. Looking back, being shaken down by these guys, as frustrating as it was, was a great opportunity to search within my company to find a solution. If it wouldn't have been for these guys, our family may have still been selling the same way, in the same place, and may not even be in business anymore.

Another lesson I learned is to always keep yourself composed, even when you are faced with injustice, harassment, or downright bullying. These guys were relentless when they came after me. They would show up at my shop, threaten me, my family, our legacy. I can't even repeat some of the things they said to me. As all this was happening, I kept my cool, kept my calm, and kept my composure. It paid off at the end because I was clear-headed in my search for a solution. If I would have lost my cool, I am not sure things would have turned out well for anybody including myself.

A final note. We are a family business. The first people I went to for advice were my parents. Their experience and wisdom helped me to look at the business with a long-term perspective, knowing we would continue to pass the business to future generations.

I asked Ángel how sharing his Painted Baby Story has built deeper relationships with his clients and those he serves. Here is what he shared with me.

I don't share the story, Matteo. It is still a very emotional moment for me even telling it to you forty years later. I do not like to think about it; I do not like to talk about it. However, telling it to you was somewhat healing for me. I realized how much resentment I have held onto for many years for the way our family was treated by these guys. Telling it also helped me realize that I addressed something that had to be

addressed for a very long time. It was one of the scariest moments of my
life; however, I would not change a thing looking back. I hope this story
helps entrepreneurs who may be facing similar struggles that I was then.

THE PAINTED BABY SOLUTION PROCESS

I hope these stories stir up some emotions that at the end of the day
ultimately push you past the doubts, or *yeah, buts,* that we talked
about in the previous chapter. I hope that now you are seeing the
benefits of sharing your story. Although these different business
owners came from different backgrounds, different industries, and
different countries, and they all had different situations, they show
that their PBS is unique and theirs, just as yours is uniquely yours.

This book is not just about the business-client relationship. It's
about paying attention to all the people whose lives are impacted by
your business, and also by you. It's about understanding your responsibility as a business owner, to lead people and build culture. Some
of these Painted Baby Stories were client-facing; others were internal team member facing; others were leadership, culture, and legacy
building focused. One story was about a business owner standing up
to adversity and blackmail and finding a solution to save his business.

Each business owner, though their situations were very different,
went through the same general process to deal with it. You may currently be facing a Painted Baby Story or situation. You may not be
ready to tell the story yet because you are still in the process of dealing with the story, the screw up, or the business blunder at hand. As
we explore the stories of these three brave entrepreneurs who shared
them, they all share common threads of how they handled their

Painted Baby moments. I like to call this the Painted Baby Solution Process. These are a list of some simple steps to remember to follow not if, but when, your Painted Baby moment arrives.

Step 1: Understand the severity of the situation. In my case as well as the case of other Painted Baby Stories in this book, there was a lot on the line, a lot to be lost, a lot to be damaged, a lot to be affected. One key in being a great business leader is to understand the severity of the situation.

Step 2: Take full ownership of the situation. Much of the advice given by these storytellers came down to taking ownership and full ownership of the situation at hand. Whether the issue at hand is your fault or not it is now yours to take ownership of.

Step 3: Make sure others are okay. This step is an important one and can easily be overlooked. Many minds immediately go into action and solution mode, and we can easily forget that whatever just happened involves people. Take time to ensure that any people involved in the situation and story are okay. If they are not, take the time to make sure they are attended to until they are okay.

Step 4: Find a solution and take action. One of the consistent themes in all these stories was the action taken by entrepreneurs. The action taken was not an over-emotionalized reaction, but rather a solution-focused response. This is a great place to ask for proper help if you need it. Remember, you do not need to go at this alone. Seek advice and input from others, especially if this situation is a new one for you.

Step 5: Ensure the action solves the problem. Many times, we take action yet forget to understand if the action solved the problem at hand. Make sure in this step that you are taking appropriate action and that your proposed solution actually solves the issue at hand.

Step 6: Evaluate and prevent. I never want to paint another baby again. Terri Coomer never wants to hear that an employee stole from one of her clients. Chris Bruno never wants to hear his organization is out of money. Ángel Fuentes Moreno never wants to be shaken down by the Sevillian tour guide mafia again. Evaluating the cause of your situation and putting measures in place to ensure it never happens again is a crucial step of the process.

Step 7: Communicate and follow up. In this step, it is important that you communicate with your team, clients, and anybody involved how you worked through the above steps. Declare that you understand the severity of the situation, voice your claim of ownership of it, and explain how you are checking on your people. Be clear and explain the action taken and proposed solution as well and follow up to explain if your solution worked. Explain clearly what measures will be taken to prevent things like this from happening moving forward.

Experiencing and addressing your first PBS will be scary, nerve-racking, and chaotic. Depending on the situation at hand, who it affects, and how it presents and plays out, things may seem out of control and not able to be managed. Please keep these steps in mind as you approach and address the issue at hand. I hope they inspire you and give you some practical tools to address your story when it comes about.

CHAPTER 13

LIFE IS BUSINESS, BUSINESS IS LIFE

As I wrote this book, I had the opportunity to hear the stories of so many entrepreneurs. Listening to their stories of courage, bravery, vulnerability, and humility while facing their struggles, challenges, nightmares, and outright awful days in business was nothing less than inspiring. After hearing their stories and realizing these lessons, I reflected back on my story as a business owner, a man, a husband, a father, and a human interacting with and serving other humans. As we jump into this chapter, I challenge and encourage you to consider these points as they relate to your business, your life, and your story.

HOW STORIES CROSS THE BRIDGE BETWEEN BUSINESS AND LIFE

I wasn't always a business owner from Colorado. I actually started life in New Jersey. An energetic kid who could never sit down or shut up, I hung out with other kids who didn't fit in much and who seemed to get in a lot of trouble. I could see myself heading in the same direction, but my parents moved out west, pulling me out of that environment and into a safer life with more positive opportunities. Many of my friends from New Jersey have died, gone to prison, or simply disappeared. But at ten years old, I started fifth grade in Northern Colorado and never looked back.

I wasn't the smartest kid or the best-looking either. My buck teeth and overbite didn't help, and neither did the headgear that I wore to correct them. Lots of kids made fun of how I looked, and I found solace not in drugs, alcohol, or any of the other destructive behaviors that many kids turn to, but in work and business. I shoveled snow, mowed lawns, and was always the number one salesperson during magazine-selling contests at school. Business and sales were my thing. Looking back, business and making money were one of the first things that gave me deep validation and confidence in myself. In college, I joined a national college painting company, earning more than $100,000 over four years. In the process, I learned a heck of a lot about the residential house painting business. College degrees in hand and ready to conquer the professional world, I looked forward to getting out of the painting business and into a suit. No more ladders for me—I was headed for a desk position and a big paycheck. I didn't know exactly what kind of work I'd be doing, but it sure wouldn't involve manual, unsexy, blue-collar work like painting houses.

I should add here that as much as I knew about painting and business, I knew little about personal finance. I had no budget and had fallen into a habit of spending more than I made. So, after purchasing a brand-new car in 2002, an overleveraged condo in 2003, getting married in 2004, I was the not-so-proud owner of $172,000 of debt.

Fortunately, I landed a position in the mortgage industry—just the kind of respectable work I had dreamed of that could put me on easy street. Wearing a button-down dress shirt, a $200 suit, and $40 tie every day felt weird for the T-shirt and jeans kind of guy I was, but it was the uniform of the industry, and of the very conservative bank that hired me.

Unfortunately, I hated the work. Being a mortgage loan officer wasn't me. It wasn't my clothes, and it wasn't how I worked. It wasn't what I wanted to do with my life. Sitting at a desk, trying to meet goals that meant nothing to me, that were set by people who didn't even know me, was like being in hell. Sure, the pay was great. It was what I needed to make my upside-down condo payments, and my car payments, and pay for everything else that contributed to my not-so-lavish, yet still costly lifestyle. Secretly, I vowed to get out of it. I remember having coffee with a good friend of mine, explaining to him that I was plotting my escape, and that it would be coming soon. However, I did not know where I would be headed next. All I did know was I would be leaving the bank and would do so on my own terms.

Six months into the position, the bank hired a new president of the mortgage division. On a Tuesday morning in March 2005, he called me into his office.

"Hey, Chad," I said, pulling up a chair. "What's up?"

"Don't sit down," he said. "This won't take long."

Huh, I thought. I had no idea what was going on. It was a typical Tuesday morning at the office. Meetings like this one never really happened and were out of the normal boring routine of the bank. I was in my usual suit-and-tie uniform, and so was Chad. Everything was perfectly normal. So, what came next was, well, kind of a shock.

"Get all your shit and put it in a box. You're fired."

I stood there for a moment, in absolute shock, waiting for his words to register. *Was this guy really firing me?*

"Maybe you should go back to that painting thing," he added with a large and condescending smirk.

Chad was sitting. I was standing, and I was so angry! Not only had I just been kicked in the gut and fired, but I also got what felt like an additional kick right between the legs after I was already down. *That painting thing. Huh*, I thought to myself, *maybe I should go back to that painting thing...*

I stormed out of Chad's office and into mine. I angrily grabbed and threw all of my belongings into a cardboard banker's box. I grabbed my pens, calculator, family photos—I even grabbed the custom business card holder plaque with the bank's logo that had my name engraved in it.

Did I mention I was pissed? As I was packing my box up, I was loudly sharing what I thought of Chad and his decision to fire me and treat me with absolutely no humanity. On the way out the door, I said goodbye to my coworkers, many of whom had become my friends. As I stormed past Chad's office, I gave him a one-finger salute and goodbye as well as hurled all of the four-letter words I knew at him. I kicked open the front door of the bank office and walked through it.

As I stepped out of the bank and onto the sidewalk curb that Tuesday morning, I immediately felt the sun shining on my face. I spent a minute and took in a couple of big breaths. I also looked up to the sky, letting the sun continue to shine down on me. The sky was clear and blue, and there was not a cloud anywhere in sight. As pissed as I was that Chad forced me out of the bank, I didn't want to be there. I was planning to leave anyway. Chad just did me a huge favor. Admittedly, I am a little bit of a control freak and wanted to leave on my own terms and time. Chad just sped up this timeline and did it in a way letting me know how significant he thought he was and how insignificant he thought I was.

Once I let the situation set in a little more, I began to respond to it rather than react to it. When this began, I realized that I had the option and opportunity to support my family and build our future doing whatever I chose. Standing there on the curb, I felt my anger, frustration, and fear turn to appreciation, excitement, and hope. I then realized I was still standing right outside the bank door I just kicked open, staring up at the sky, breathing deeply, and holding a banker's box.

I made three vows at that moment.

First, I loosened the tie from around my neck, removed it, and threw it in the trash can. I vowed never to wear a tie again to work. Second, I vowed that I would never work for anybody like Chad again. Third, I vowed I would never work for anybody again, period. In that moment I declared with absolute certainty that I am an entrepreneur; I am meant to be an entrepreneur and I was ready to step into this journey as an entrepreneur.

I then took a step from the sidewalk curb outside the bank door into the parking lot. I will remember this moment and this step for the rest of my life. That step signified the beginning of my official journey into business. That step signified the birth of M & E Painting. That step signified freedom, purpose, and passion. Looking back, that step taught and showed me so many things that I would like to share with you in this chapter.

I jumped into my car and began the drive home, which was just twelve minutes long. During those twelve minutes, I was contemplating how I would break the news to Emily that I was just fired. *What would she think? How would she react?* I was about to find out.

"Honey, I'm home" I stated as I walked through the front door.

"You are home early today, Matt. What's up?" she asked.

"Chad fired me!" I replied.

I was terrified. I was also determined to support our family and create our future together. After she had a minute to take it all in, I could see the fear and concern but also the support in her eyes. Without skipping a beat, she replied, "I believe in you, you've got this, and I have your back no matter what." She then asked, "What are you going to do about it?"

I replied, "I'm starting a painting company and I need to head out RIGHT NOW to get to work. We need to make $2,800 in 28 days."

That year, I made more money painting houses than I had the whole four years in college. I made more than I had working for Chad. M & E Painting closed out its first nine months with half a million dollars in top-line revenue. The next year, we did $800,000 and in 2007, we topped $1.2 million. Within four years of starting the business, we were doing more than $2 million a year in revenue.

Back then, I looked at every client and every project as another step up the million-dollar mountain. I didn't see the people whose homes I painted as *people*—people with lives, with stories. I didn't even see my own story. Focused solely on money and success, I missed out on the most important part of business: the people.

I was being a Chad.

I had bought into the idea that a successful life was about making money and looking good to the rest of the world. It wasn't about our story, others' stories, and building meaningful relationships and connections with others. To me, success was directly related to my bottom line and that was it. I would never dream of being vulnerable, weak, and just plain human. I woke up every day in my painting company to make money as I painted not only homes but painted a picture of perfection.

I didn't like telling those stories about painting the right house the wrong color and almost painting the wrong house the right color. I wanted to pretend those things never happened. Like I never struggled. I never got fired from a job (even one I hated). And I never made any mistakes in my painting business. For the longest time, I kept those stories to myself. And I insulated myself from the most important part of business—the people.

That day in Bill's office, opening up about my worst stories, taught me a valuable lesson that changed the way I did business. I learned that my stories—the best ones, the worst ones, and most of all, the best worst ones—were the key to breaking down the barriers between myself and the people with whom I needed to connect. My team. My clients. Other people in my life too, outside of business.

I've never worn a tie to work since that day I walked out of the bank. I still buy all my clothes at Kohl's and rarely spend more than a hundred bucks from head to toe. I'm comfortable in my sneakers, comfortable in my skin, and comfortable knowing that the people I spend the most time with know me—the good, the bad, and the ugly—and they still stick by me. I don't hide anything anymore and it hasn't made me weak. It's strengthened me and my business. Most importantly, it's strengthened my relationships with the most important thing in business, in the world: people.

I ran into Chad again in 2019. After my painting business, I launched a number of other companies and also became a realtor. One Saturday afternoon, Chad was interested in a house I had listed for sale. I was hosting an open house at this property, and he stopped by to take a tour. As he entered the home, he looked at me blankly, like I was just another real estate agent. Didn't bat an eye. He didn't recognize me. That's when it hit home: guys like Chad really *don't* see people. I had been nothing more than a number to him. Firing me meant absolutely nothing more to him than an adjustment on his P&L report. I was at the open house to gauge interest and connect with people, and Chad was not interested. He was completely disengaged, self-absorbed, and arrogant, just as much as he had been in 2005 when he fired me.

Telling my Painted Baby Story was one of the most honest things I've ever done, and it changed who I was in business and in life. It made me more aware of the importance of being honest with who I was and being a person who I was proud to be. That meant treating people with respect and dignity and expecting them to reciprocate by treating me the same way. That is what I deserved, what we all deserve when we're willing to show the world who we really are.

Vulnerability is every bit as important in business as it is in your personal life. I've said it before, and I'll say it again: business is just humans serving other humans. In business, we invest our time, talents, and treasures into others to bring value to their life, and in turn we get something out of it. In any other relationship that involves people, the same thing happens. In marriage, friendship, and volunteer work, we invest in others and there is something we receive in return. Life is business and business is life. It is important that we show up as the most real and honest version of ourselves to help and inspire others to improve their lives. Any time we show up less than that, we shortchange ourselves and our potential to connect with others. In doing so, we underserve those we are here to help.

When you have impactful and memorable moments in your business—both good and bad—you share them with those in your life. For instance, I remember the first real estate deal I closed. After signing the paperwork, I was on cloud nine. I came home and immediately shared with Emily. Similarly, when we painted the baby, Emily was the first person I told. It was a bad day, and there was no way I could keep an incident like that from affecting me personally. I had to tell my wife. The same rings true when we have an impactful and memorable moment personally, either good or bad; this will affect us and be brought into business.

Being honest about who you are in business will affect who you are in the rest of your life. If you're a shiny marketing brochure at work, chances are, you may be acting the same with your loved ones at home. Early on, I knew I was—I painted a picture of perfection in my marriage, my faith, my business, and my relationships. I tried to force myself into different boxes. At work, I was Business Matt. At home, I was Dad Matt to my son and daughter. I was Friend Matt, Spouse Matt...you get the picture. When I did this, I felt like I had to show up in thirteen different ways for thirteen different parts of my life.

How about you? Do you feel pressure to change hats and show up differently to the different people you serve in your life? Do you compartmentalize your true self only revealing it to some people or possibly no people at all? Are you worried that others may judge you or change their perception of you if and when you expose your true self?

Once I pulled those partitions back and decided to just be real and *me* in all parts of my life, life became so much easier. I chose to carry my values and my true self with me everywhere.

The kicker in all of this is that my business wasn't the only thing that got better once I started sharing my PBS. My whole life changed. I relaxed. I stopped worrying if I was perfect enough for every relationship and situation. I stopped being all those different Matts and just became *Matt*. Me. This guy who isn't perfect, but he's good enough. And that Matt, *this* guy, is a lot happier. I like him better. Other people like him—like *me*—better too.

How will your life change when you tell your Painted Baby Story? What would you like to change? How will your business change? What will your relationships be like when people see the brave, vulnerable you?

QUESTIONS TO CONSIDER

1. How has a recent impactful and memorable life event carried over into your business?

2. How has a recent impactful and memorable business event carried over into your life?

3. Do you feel like you are compartmentalizing yourself into business, family, and personal boxes? If so, how can you remove these barriers?

4. Consider all of the hats you wear and domains of your life that you show up to. What are the common threads of the true you that shows up to all of them? Is the real you not showing up to any of them?

CONCLUSION

We have taken a long journey together. Thank you for taking it and for trusting me to guide you and walk alongside you. Thank you for listening to my story, but more importantly the stories of so many brave and vulnerable small business leaders who contributed to this book. As we near the end of this book, I hope you have been challenged to consider how you are currently approaching your business, the stories you tell, and the communication you have with your clients and those you serve. I also hope you've been encouraged and inspired to consider the power of stories (especially yours) and to consider a new way of telling your story, building relationships, and marketing your business. I hope, like me, you're reconsidering the messages you're putting out into the world and asking yourself if you could do better. I hope you grab hold of and implement this useful and effective framework to capture, craft, and communicate not just any story, but a deeper story, a more vulnerable story, a more imperfect and impactful story. With this, I also hope you ultimately create truer, better, more meaningful connections with the people in your life.

I hope you come away from this book with a better understanding of the many voices that can keep you from telling your story, where they come from, and what to do with them. Consider the voices you take in, making sure they serve you, instead of silencing you. Trust yourself and find the courage to test and tell your story.

Capture, craft, and communicate your story privately and then publicly. Don't shy away from recrafting it—pay attention to the responses you get when you tell your story and learn to make it clearer, sharper, better.

There is no finish line to telling your story. It will continue to evolve as you share it and discover new connections that your story has to other people and other situations. In the process of writing this book, I learned more about my Painted Baby Story and how it impacted my life and business.

You will doubt your story. You might doubt yourself. I did. But you're a leader, and I know you have the courage to go first by telling your PBS—when you are ready. Don't be held hostage by your fears, and don't ignore your concerns. Look at them and see them for what they are: some will be real, but many will be imaginary barriers to exposing your vulnerability.

By this point, you can see how business and life are not separate. Business is simply a formalized version of humans serving other humans. You cannot run a business without serving other people. The most valuable and precious servitude requires trust between humans, and it is through honest and authentic storytelling that trust is created and continues to flourish.

Remember, you only get one story. Tell it well. Tell it with bravery and courage. Dig deep; be vulnerable. Allow others to see you for who you truly are and be sure to see them for who they truly are.

Everybody has a Painted Baby Story. Are you ready to share yours with the world?

Flip to the About the Author page for my website and other ways to contact me. I want to hear your story. I am excited to hear your story. I am also looking forward to helping you discover the deep power within your story, all of it, so that you can connect deeper and more frequently with others in your business and life.

I am here for you, and I have your back. I want you to know that. I love you. I believe in you. You've got this. Now go get it.

ACKNOWLEDGMENTS

There are so many people whom I appreciate and would like to acknowledge and thank. Each one of them has contributed to my entrepreneurial journey, my life journey, and to the development and publishing of this book.

First and foremost, thank you Jesus for coming into my life, grabbing hold of my life, guiding, and directing my life and walking with me through life.

I want to thank my wife, Emily, and my children, Riley and Hailey. You have been the most important part of my life journey. I love you three with all my heart. You make me a better man and a better person and have encouraged me while watching me develop throughout this process, especially supporting me when I decided to finish this book.

I would also like to thank Emily's parents, Steve and Carrie, for their continued encouragement and unflagging belief in me over the years.

My business journey wouldn't be the same without all of the Sevilla Holdings team members who have served all of our companies. Thank you for your time, investment, dedication, and faith in me and our company to provide for you and your family. Thank you all for your words of encouragement, support, and your belief in me to continue to pursue my journey as an author.

A todos mis amigos y familiares en España, seamos familia de sangre o no, os considero familia. Vuestro país, vuestra cultura y las relaciones que mantengo con vosotros han sido una parte muy importante de mi vida, de mi historia y de mi crecimiento. Algunas de mis mejores ideas, reflexiones y conclusiones sobre dónde debo estar y qué debo hacer han ocurrido mientras pasaba tiempo en vuestro hermoso país. Os quiero a todos.

María del Mar López Cabrales, gracias por tu amistad y por el ánimo que me has dado para visitar España. Eres la responsable de toda la pasión que tengo por España. Ha sido un placer seguir nuestra amistad durante todos estos años.

Thank you to all my jiu jitsu training partners. As we step on the mats together, we push and challenge each other to improve every day. The process of doing that and the relationships that I have with you all has pushed me to zones of discomfort that I've never experienced before. The mental, physical, and psychological aspect of what we do together was a huge driving force behind knowing that I could not only complete this book but get it in the hands of as many people as possible.

Thank you to Ruth Rennie, my second-grade teacher. Thank you for your belief and words of encouragement in me as a child. You believed in me and loved me when many others did not. I have so much enjoyed our continued friendship over the past thirty years.

Thanks to Bill Scott for your continued support and belief in me. This book may have never come to life if it were not for that meeting in your office years ago.

Thank you to the authors, speakers, and thought leaders whom I've built relationships with throughout the years. In particular, thank you to Mike Michalowicz. You've been a huge inspiration. Thank you for challenging me to commit to being an author.

Thank you to the wonderful people who contributed their stories in this book.

Rick Scadden, it is an honor to know you and be a part of your journey and story. I am excited to read your book one day.

Dave Sanderson, thank you for your friendship and continued words of encouragement over the years.

Dave Albin, thank you for your friendship and for the work you have done with me and my team. Your words of encouragement and motivation were very impactful to me as I wrote this book.

Terri Coomer, thank you so much for sharing your story and for connecting again with me after all these years.

Chris Bruno, I am so thankful to you and for you for so many reasons. Thank you for your friendship, your story, and your contribution to my life and my journey as a man.

Really Cool Contractor, thank you for allowing me to be one of the first people to hear your story. It is a powerful and inspiring one. I hope you decide to share it with many more people.

Ángel Fuentes Moreno, gracias por tu amistad, tu apoyo y tu historia. Es un honor y un placer haberte conocido a ti y a tu familia. Tenemos muchos recuerdos entrañables con vosotros y estoy seguro de que vendrán muchos más en un futuro.

Thank you to everyone at Scribe. Your team was amazing to work with and brought *Painted Baby* to life. I appreciate and thank every single one of you.

To anybody who I haven't thanked or mentioned, but who has come into my life for any amount of time and inspired me, encouraged me, and challenged me to be better—in a big or small way— thank you for being a part of my life.

ABOUT THE AUTHOR

MATT SHOUP is an award-winning serial entrepreneur and is passionate about inspiring business owners to discover their leadership potential. He is the founder of M & E Painting, M & E Roofing Solutions, M & E Real Estate Ventures, MattShoup.com, Shoup Commercial, and Sevilla Holdings. He is also the co-founder of Northern Colorado Jiu Jitsu and RiRy, makers of the Pirate Patch® Drywall Repair Tool. Matt also founded and created *The Gentle Art of Leadership*™, a personal and professional leadership development program, and *The Ultimate Immersion Experience*, an experiential leadership retreat to Spain.

Matt was recognized by *ColoradoBiz Magazine* as one of the "Top Five Most Influential Young Professionals in Colorado" in 2010 and by *Northern Colorado Business Report* as one of "40 Under 40 Top Business Leaders in Northern Colorado" in 2013. He was named "Alumni of the Last Decade" in 2012 by Colorado State University, receiving the college's Gold Award.

M & E Painting was named one of the "United States Top Small Workplaces" by "Winning Workplaces" and *Inc. Magazine* in 2012, and one of Colorado's Top 250 Privately Owned Companies in Colorado by *ColoradoBiz Magazine* in 2010. M & E Painting was on the list of *Inc. Magazine*'s "5,000 Fastest-Growing Companies in the US" in 2010 and received the "Northern Colorado Better Business Bureau Torch Award for Ethics" in 2017. M & E Painting has also appeared on *NOCO Style Magazine*'s "Northern Colorado's Best Of" list for six out of the last seven years.

Matt and his wife, Emily, cofounded the "Matt and Emily Shoup Spain Study Abroad Scholarship" through Colorado State University. To date, this scholarship has sent sixteen students to Spain to study abroad. Matt continues to grow that scholarship through his passion project and free coffee bar, *Café Sevilla* (www.cafesevillacoffeebar.com).

Matt received his Brazilian Jiu Jitsu black belt from Master Rigan Machado in August 2020. He has competed in Brazilian Jiu Jitsu tournaments both in Spain and the United States and enjoys spending time teaching his students who attend Northern Colorado Jiu Jitsu. He is also an author, bilingual keynote speaker, philanthropist, Realtor, Spain aficionado, Spanish coffee addict, and aspiring paella chef. His first book, *Become an Award-Winning Company*, published in 2011, is a guide for business owners teaching them how to win business awards and leverage them to grow their companies and brands.

Matt lives in Northern Colorado with his wife, Emily, their children, Riley and Hailey, and their giant schnoodle, Romeo. To connect with Matt, whether it's to talk about Spain, share a coffee, share business and/or life stories, or for keynote speaking, book signing, or coaching inquiries, reach out at www.mattshoup.com. You can also find him on social media.

Facebook: https://www.facebook.com/matt.shoup

Instagram: https://www.instagram.com/matthewshoup

LinkedIn: https://www.linkedin.com/in/mattshoup

YouTube: https://www.youtube.com/c/MattShoup

Twitter: https://twitter.com/MattShoup

TikTok: https://www.tiktok.com/@mattshoup